The Streets *of* Dayton, Texas

History by the Block

Caroline Wadzeck

The History Press

Published by The History Press
Charleston, SC 29403
www.historypress.net

Front cover, top left: Courtesy of the Illustrated Magazine, *Liberty, Texas; top right: Courtesy of Liberty County Central Appraisal District. Back cover, lower: Courtesy of Suzanne Sellers, muralist.*

First published 2014

Manufactured in the United States

ISBN 978.1.62619.473.1

Library of Congress CIP data applied for.

Courtesy Barbara Harris.

Dedicated to
Robert D. "Bobby" Harris
1921–2013
A lifelong Dayton resident and community leader who had a wealth of knowledge about Dayton's history

CONTENTS

Acknowledgements 9
Introduction 11

A–G
Aaron Street 15
Atascocita 16
Barrow Street 17
Beauty Street 18
Benton Street 18
Brooks Street 20
Brown Road 21
Brown Trail 23
Bryan Street 23
Cherry Creek Road 25
Chester Street 28
Church Street 29
Clarence Street 35
Clayton Street 36
Cleveland Street and State Highway 321 37
Colbert Street 40
Coleman Street 41
Collins Street 42
Daisy Street 44

Dale Street	45
Depot Street	46
Edgar Street	48
Elaine Street	49
Emma Street	50
Entzminger Street	52
Esther Street	53
Evelyn Street	54
Flowers Street	55
FM Highway 1960	56
Ford Avenue	57
Fordland Estates	58
Friery Street	60
Glass Street	61
Goosecreek Street	61

H–M

Harmon Street	63
Hickory Lane	64
Hill Street	64
Hillcrest	65
Holbrook Street	65
Holitzke Street	67
Holmes Street	68
Houston Street	68
Hunnicutt Street	69
Jamison Street	70
Juanita Street	72
Kay Street	73
Kerr Street	74
Kindt Street	75
Klemp Road	76
LaBlanc Lane	77
LaCour Street	79
Ladd Street	79
Laird Street	82
Lawrence Street	82
Ligons Street	85
Linney Street	86

Lisa Lane	87
Little John	88
Lovers Lane	88
Lowe Street	89
Luke Street	90
Main Street	91
Manor Street	93
Marblehead Street	93
McBride Street	95
Meadows Lane	95
Meremar Lane	96
Merritt Street	98
Milo Street	98
Mockingbird Lane	100
Moller Street	101
Myra Lane	101
N–Z	
Nancy Street	103
Nelton Street	103
Norcross Lane	105
Oak Street	107
Park Place	108
Paul Street	109
Pecan Street	110
Pine Place	110
Pine Street	110
Prater Street	110
Pruitt Street	111
Ranchwood	113
River Oaks	113
Ross Street	113
Sawmill Road	115
Seaberg Industrial Road	115
Seekamp Street	117
Shanks Street	118
Sherwood Drive	120
Skylark	120
Slover Drive	121

Smith Street	122
State Highway 146	123
Sterling Street	125
Stevens Street	129
Stone Street	131
Sunset Heights	132
Susan Street	132
Taylor Lane	133
Timber Lane	134
Tram Road	135
Tucker Street	136
U.S. Highway 90 (Old Spanish Trail)	137
Waco Street	141
Waring Street	143
Westwood Street	144
Whitewing	145
Willow Street	145
Winfree	145
Young Street	147
Zylks Road	148
Historic Main Street Businesses	151
Notes	155
Index	175
About the Author	191

ACKNOWLEDGEMENTS

I want thank the following people for their help with the information for this book:

Lena Ruth Dearbonne Allen
Boyd and Patsie Arnold
Ted Boyer
Terry Boyett
Percy Brooks
Dale Brown
Don Brown
Eleanor Brown
Gene Brown
Norman Brown
Sandra Burrell
Donna Carouthers
John Collins
Alan Dee and Mary Ellen Conner
Iris Collins Eaton
Pomella Eaton
Lillie Flowers
M.W. Ford Jr.
Mary Strickland Fregia
Saul Friedman
Burly Ligons Gant
Lisa Wilson Gibson
Bernice Green
Shirley Haidusek
Sharon Harbors
Lynne Lowe Harding
Bobby Harris
Larry and Linda Harris
Aaron Holbrook
Betty LeBlanc Holitzke
Linda Jamison
Mary Beth Jamison
Bill and Norma Johnson
John and Jessica Johnson
Curtis Laird
Sherial Lawson
Mary LeBlanc
Annette Lockett

Debbie Martin
Kathryn Martin
Sue Moore
Darlene Mott
Mutt Neuman
E.B. Neuman II
Dovie Norcross
Zoe Norcoss
Sue Park
David Parker
Joann Paul
Lloyd Pierce
Susan Wilson Potetz
Hurley Provost
Lois Pruitt
Alphene Richter
Sonny and Tish Richter
Amy Ripkowski
Bobby Sanders
Carl Sanders
Susan Seaberg
Punky Moreau Shanks
Kevin Sheffield
Sonny Smith
Betty Sterling
Jimmy Sterling
Adelene Stevens
Eileen Stoesser
Howard and Dollie Stone
Gayle Taylor
Tom Tucker
Mary Turner
Sandra Voytek
Larry Wadzeck
Lester Ray and Betty Jo Wisegerber
Nell Norcross Whittington
Betty Sterling Williamson
Laura Wilson
Annie Wingo
Bobbie Zylks

INTRODUCTION

In 1757, all of Southeast Texas was known as Atascosito. Because several important roads joined at what is now present-day Liberty and the Trinity River was navigable at this point, the potentials of the area were quickly realized by would-be settlers. When the area was opened to Anglo colonization by the Spanish, settlers advanced in a steady stream. By the late 1820s, the residents of the area, hoping to receive land titles and desiring to become part of Austin's Colony, saw that it was necessary to determine the population of the district as a means of gaining their objectives.

Therefore, in 1826, the first census recorded in Texas—referred to as the Atascosito Census—was taken by Matthew G. White, Joseph W. Brown, George Orr and Henry W. Munson, several of the earliest Anglo settlers of the area. The town that became known as Liberty, founded in 1831, was located on the four-league Mexican land grant appropriated for the capital of the old municipality of Santísima Trinidad de la Libertad. The town of Liberty was divided by the Trinity River, with the section on the east side called Liberty and the section located on a hill west of the river called West Liberty. Both sections were considered part of the original town, directly connected by a road and ferry.

Sometime after 1854, West Liberty also became known as Day's Town or Daystown, for I.C. Day, a wealthy landowner who resided south of the town on the Munson League. The flag stop for the Texas and New Orleans Railroad, completed in 1860, was known variously as West Liberty, Days Station and Dayton Station. The name Dayton was applied to the local post office in 1877, though the official name of the town remained West Liberty until the mid-1880s.

In 1885, Dayton reported a population of 60, and in 1890, a post office, a school and two churches served 239 residents. Lumbering and cattle raising were the chief industries until James E. Berry helped establish a drainage system to make rice a major crop. In 1905, the Dayton Lumber Company was organized, beginning operation in 1906 and employing 250 people. This company was instrumental in the early development of Dayton. By 1910, the town had a bank, two cotton gins, a weekly newspaper and 2,500 inhabitants.

As reported by the *Liberty Vindicator* on February 17, 1911, "At the election holden at Dayton last Friday to determine whether or not that township should be incorporated, the question carried by a vote of: for incorporation 80; against incorporation 57." For reasons unknown, city records show that Dayton was reincorporated in November 1925.

Oil development during the 1920s brought new industries. By 1940, Dayton had seventy businesses and was listed as a railroad center. The population increased steadily from 3,367 in 1965 to 6,201 in 1988. In 1989, the largest school population in the county made the Dayton Independent School District the major employer in the city. By 1990, Dayton had a population of 5,151; in 2000, the population was 5,709; and in 2012, the number had risen to 7,337.

A comprehensive book about the history of Dayton has yet to be written, but rather than doing more research on the town of Dayton, I became interested in researching its street names. My desire to do this project arose after attending the Texas Library Association Conference in Houston in 2011. Each evening after a day at the conference, my librarian friends and I would share the books we had bought at the exhibit area. My friend Anna Mae Veach, library coordinator at Hardin Independent School District, purchased a book entitled *Historic Streets of Houston* by Mark Hinton. Curious about some of the street names, I began to read. As I read, I thought about Dayton, where I live, and wondered who some of those streets were named for. The more I thought about it, the more I was interested in finding out, and a research project was born.

Initially, I thought I would simply find out for whom Dayton's streets are named, but that idea quickly grew into my wanting to know as much as possible about each person and also what they looked like. I found that many of the people have been deceased for years, and sadly, some lived so long ago that there is no one left alive who remembers who they were.

A project of this nature involves research in the usual places—libraries, the county courthouse, museums, the appraisal district and the Internet—but it also involves talking to numerous people who have direct knowledge of the information one is seeking. Many of the people I interviewed were of advanced age and have/had lived in Dayton for most—if not all—of their lives. I met and talked with many interesting people in order to piece together this part of Dayton's history.

At some point, it became clear to me that I would also include streets not only named for people but also that are part of Dayton's history, such as Church Street, Depot Street, Main Street, etc. They, too, have their own stories worth telling.

I had hoped to include every Dayton street but was unable to find information for them all. That catchy theme song for the television program CSI, "Who Are You" by The Who, ran through my head as I searched in vain for answers to several street names. Those are listed below, and if any reader has definite information about them, please contact me. In researching Dayton's streets, I have learned a lot about the history of my town and how unique its street names are.

Streets for which no information could be found: Austin, Bell, Calvin, Carl, Cook, Dalhart, Dunlo, Glendale, Hope, Larson, Mitchell, Pearl and Tyler.

Caroline Wadzeck
cwadzeck@hotmail.com
P.O. Box 459
Dayton, Texas 77535

A–G

Aaron Street

Aaron Street is named for Aaron Chester Holbrook Sr. and is located in the Holbrook subdivision that he created in 1962 (see Chester Street and Holbrook Street). Known as Chester, he was born in Liberty County on March 12, 1900, to George and Annie Holbrook. His family later moved to Pasadena, where they grew strawberries on a twenty-acre farm. He attended school first in Pasadena and then bicycled five miles a day to Milby High School in Harrisburg, until the district finally got a school bus.

Finishing high school in 1917, Chester attended Texas A&M for two years while he studied civil engineering. He also learned how to repair his own machinery while there. Holbrook began his rice-farming career with Joe Nelson near Dayton in 1920 when rice farming was done with a one-seat sulky plow pulled by four mules. In an interview published in the *Liberty Vindicator* in 1982, he remembered that in his early days as a rice farmer, a lot of the work had to be done by hand. Rice was planted with an end gate seeder and a rice drill. The rice was cut with binders and put in shocks to dry for about twenty days, and then it was thrashed.

Chester married Ellen Nelson in 1922. She had moved to Dayton from Iowa with her parents, Carl David and Anna Nelson, when she was two years old. Her father was one of the early rice farmers in Dayton. Chester

Aaron Chester Holbrook. *Courtesy of the* Liberty Vindicator.

and Ellen raised six children: A.C. Jr., Bruce R., Evelyn (Waldrop), Juanita (Rizzo), Virgil "Buddy" and John David.

One of Chester's early interests was flying airplanes, and he purchased his first plane when flying was in its infancy. His second plane burned up. In the 1982 *Vindicator* interview, he said, "I learned to fly by flying with first one and then another. Nobody would go up with me, so I just cranked it up and flew it."

Chester built the first rice dryer in Dayton on the corner on Highway 321 and Clayton Street. A contractor for many years, he and partner Will Graves built the current highway route from Dayton to Barbers Hill (FM 146), other roads in Montgomery County and one airport at Anahuac and another in Lake Charles, Louisiana.

In the early 1960s, he became a Lone Star Beer distributor in Dayton, co-owning the distributorship with Ellis Taylor (see Taylor Lane article). He was a member of the Masonic Lodge.[1] Chester died on February 21, 1990,[2] preceded by his wife, Ellen, who passed away in 1987.[3] They are buried at Magnolia Park Cemetery in Dayton. Many of their descendants still reside in Dayton.

Atascocita

This is one of the streets in the Linney Creek subdivision. Prior to being a subdivision, the land was a dairy farm owned by a man named Peterson who sold the four hundred acres to Roy and Myra Slover in 1955. The Slovers bought the land as an investment and, for years, would drive over from their home in Liberty to enjoy their creek house and let their dogs run about. According to Ted Boyer, who was a part-time employee, business associate and friend of Roy and Myra, he helped them lay out the streets in the subdivision in the late 1960s or '70s. The Slovers named all of the streets at that time, with the first to develop named Slover Street. It is not definitely known why the Slovers chose Atascocita for the street name, but since that Spanish word means "boggy" or "soft and watery," the name fits well, as the area incorporates a creek and is very boggy after a big rain.[4]

See the Slover Street and Myra Street sections for more information.

Barrow Street

Douglas Barrow. *Courtesy of the* Liberty Vindicator.

This is one of eleven streets renamed by the Dayton City Council in 1961 for Dayton servicemen killed in World War II. This street was originally called Second Avenue[5] and was renamed for Douglas Barrow, son of B.A. and Anna Barrow, who was killed in action in Germany on March 28, 1945. He was thirty-one years old. Barrow was a 1934 graduate of Dayton High School and was an outstanding player with the Dayton Bronchos for three years. He was employed by the Shell Oil Company before entering the U.S. Army.

Barrow received his training at Fort Sill, Oklahoma. He was commissioned as first lieutenant there in 1943 and went overseas with the 336th Field Artillery Battalion, 87th Infantry Division, in November 1944 as an aerial observer. He held the Air Medal and two Oak Leaf Clusters and was well on his way to his third cluster, with forty-five missions to his credit. Barrow is buried at Lorraine American Cemetery in St. Avold, France.[6]

Beauty Street

Beauty Street was named in the mid-1940s when the Dayton City Council gave names to unnamed streets. The story begins in 1910 when Carl Sanders and his wife, Else Zachariah, moved to Dayton from California after emigrating from China about 1906. Else lived in China with her missionary parents, her father being a doctor. The couple married prior to their immigration to the United States.

They bought seven acres of land soon after moving to Dayton on what became Beauty Street. They raised their four children (three sons and one daughter) there, including their oldest son, Hunt, who, with his wife, Laura Lee (Wright), continued living on the home place, raising their family of three children (sons Carl and Robert "Bobby" and a daughter).

Bobby and Carl Sanders remember their mother telling them that when the city fathers began discussing a name for the street, one suggested Sanders Lane. Dr. Ernest Richter, one of the councilmen, talked about how muddy the street was and how deep the ruts would get and suggested tongue-in-cheek that they name it Beauty Street. The name stuck.[7] This was verified by Alphene Richter, Dr. Richter's wife.[8]

Some current residents on Beauty Street said they had always heard that it got its name because there were so many beautiful ladies living there. Another resident said it was because it was such an ugly street. It is today one of the best-paved concrete streets in the city and more aptly lives up to its name.

Benton Street

Benton Street was named after the Thomas J. and Eliza McLeod Benton family, who, in 1898, purchased the land on which the street is located.

Thomas was born on March 10, 1858, in Walker or Chatooga County, Georgia. His father was Jabe Harmon and his mother Mary Martha Benton. A great-granddaughter of the Bentons, Pat Landwehr, said family lore claims that Thomas's father was killed by lightning while his parents were betrothed. Benton told his grandchildren, to whom he was known as "Grandpap," that he was raised by his maternal grandfather. He also said that he and his mother, Mary Martha, moved to Etoway County, Alabama, when he was fifteen years old and "proved a homestead."

Thomas J. Benton. *Courtesy of Pat Landwehr.*

Eliza Benton. *Courtesy of Pat Landwehr.*

Eliza Elnora McLeod was born on February 11, 1858, in Roanoke, Randolph County, Alabama, to Angus and Elizabeth (Burgess) McLeod. Eliza told her children and grandchildren that she met Thomas at a country dance soon after her family moved to Marshall County and they immediately fell in love. After seeing each other three times, Thomas rode on horseback to her house to ask her father for her hand in marriage, which was given. They married on April 16, 1881, in Marshall, Alabama, and had seven children.

Eliza's brother, James Franklin McLeod, was a Baptist preacher who founded several churches in Texas and was called to be the preacher at what eventually became First Baptist Church in Dayton in 1898. He and church member W.C. Moore purchased land to construct a new church building for $1,000. Pastor McLeod urged his sister and her husband to move to Texas "for prime farm land."

Thomas and Eliza purchased land in Dayton prior to moving their family to Texas in 1900 from Gadsden County, Alabama. Even though they owned land in Dayton, the family spent several years farming in Waller County. Eliza passed away on February 23, 1928, in Dayton and is buried at Huffman Cemetery, Harris

County, Texas. The 1930 U.S. census shows Thomas living with his son Angus and family in Dayton at the age of seventy-two. He passed away on August 26, 1933, in Dayton and is also buried at Huffman Cemetery.

Angus Thomas Walter Benton, Thomas and Eliza's oldest son, was sixteen years old when the family moved to Texas. He was born on January 2, 1884, in Etowah County, Alabama. He probably met his future wife, Wessie Aldridge Goodrum, while living in Waller, for they married there on October 31, 1907.

Wessie Aldridge Goodrum was born on September 8, 1884, in Navasota, Texas, to Thomas Joseph and Fannie (Davis) Goodrum. Wessie and Angus had five children: Bruce Elbert, who died at the age of six; Roger Wayne; Marcille Elizabeth (Broussard); Caleista Weiba (Lyne); and Angus Thomas "A.T." Benton Jr.

After the Bentons moved to Dayton, Angus and his brothers farmed in the Eastgate area and sent their children to town to go to school. When Angus and Wessie retired from farming, they moved into town and built their home on Linney Cemetery Road.

Pat Landwehr said, "Grandpa Angus had a large garden—he made pocket money selling his tomatoes and watermelons. He also grafted pecan trees and was always experimenting with developing new strains. He was quite skilled at carpentry, blacksmithy, and even crafted some john boats [light boats with a flat design]." She describes her grandfather as a man with a dry sense of humor who loved his family and sang like Bing Crosby.[9]

Angus passed away on June 25, 1960, and is buried at Magnolia Park Cemetery in Dayton. He was a member of First Baptist Church, and the Reverend J.L. Jordan officiated at his funeral. His obituary states that he was a retired farmer and resided in Dayton for approximately sixty years.[10] Wessie died on June 21, 1971, and is also buried at Magnolia Park Cemetery.

Following the death of Angus, the Benton children (Roger, Marcille, Caleista and A.T.) needed to obtain funds to care for their mother, Wessie, so they decided to subdivide the property and sell lots. Benton Street came from this development.

Brooks Street

Brooks Street is named for Mr. Clarence Brooks, who was born in Broussard, Louisiana. He moved to Dayton in 1924 and married Louise Broussard in

Louise and Clarence Brooks. *Courtesy of Percy Brooks.*

1925. They had a large family that included nine children: Rachel Nora, Rubie (who died as an infant), Albert, Alfred, Annie Laura, Earnest, Percy and Henry. They lived in the Eastgate community west of Dayton and engaged in farming. About 1957, the Brooks family moved to the French Settlement in the northern part of Dayton, so named because French Creoles from Louisiana had settled there late in the nineteenth century. The "streets" in the area were in deplorable condition, and Mr. Brooks petitioned the Dayton City Council to pave them. He was very outspoken and persistent in this matter until it was done, and the street was named after him in honor of this achievement. Clarence died in 1985, preceded by his wife, who had passed away in 1965. They are buried at Ames Catholic Cemetery in Ames, Texas.[11]

Brown Road

Brown Road is named for Harry and Kimmie Brown. What is now called Brown Road was actually a forty-foot dedicated road right of way as part of the Elisabeth Munson League many years before Harry Charles Brown purchased the property along the south boundary.

Harry and Kimmie Brown. *Courtesy of Norman Brown.*

The right of way extended from FM 1409 to State Highway 146 but was never opened up as a road. When Harry purchased his property in 1939 and 1940, there was a gate at the entrance to FM 1409. A fence crossed the roadway west of Harry's property line. The road was open a short distance from State Highway 146 on the other end. Around 1956, Harry and Kimmie moved onto their property. Others began building homes from both ends of the roadway, and finally the fence was taken down to connect the two ends. At that time, it was named Brown Road and became a Liberty County road.

Born in 1899, Harry came to Dayton in 1901 as a two-year-old with his parents, Charles Sumner and Bertha Brown.The family previously lived in Iowa and, after seeing an ad placed by a land developer, decided to move to Dayton because they were looking for better farmland. The Brown family was in good company, as the Nelson and Seaberg families also moved to Dayton about the same time from the same community. Descendants of the three families still reside in Dayton.

Harry was raised with three siblings: his brother, George, and two sisters, Bertie and Olive. He attended Dayton schools, played basketball in high school and graduated in 1915 or '16. He met and fell in love with a local schoolteacher named Kimmie Meyers, and they married in 1930. Kimmie Brown Elementary School is named for her and is located where the family's home was situated.

Harry and Kimmie raised two children: Charlene and Norman. Norman remembers that as a small child in the late 1930s, he would occasionally see local Daytonite Cy Young drive his cattle down Brown Road, across FM 1409 to Ford Road, off which was a dipping vat. Norman's father, Harry, was a rancher and farmer and also raised horses. People knew they were getting a good horse when they bought from Harry Brown. Harry passed away in 1975 and Kimmie in 1991. Both are buried in Magnolia Park Cemetery in Dayton.[12]

Brown Trail

The original name of this road was Tallow Wood Trail, named by Bill Sjolander, who built the street and began the subdivision. The street was so named because of the tallow trees on the lots. The land was later acquired in 1992 by Boyd Arnold, Alan Dee Conner, Larry Harris and John Simmons, who replatted the lots to make them each three-fourths of an acre. They decided to rename the street Brown Trail since it intersected Brown Road, which was named after Harry and Kimmie Brown, who gave most of the land for the road.[13]

Bryan Street

Bryan Street had two previous names. It was first called Ambler[14] and later named Post Office Avenue.[15] It was renamed for Oliver Bryan (O.B.) Sterling Sr. The street was so named between 1961 and '63 during the time that Jim Sterling, his nephew, was mayor. Several streets were either named or renamed at that time by a committee formed by the Dayton City Council. Eleven streets were renamed for Dayton servicemen who died during World War II, and others were named after Dayton residents or people who contributed to the development of Dayton.

O.B. Sterling Sr. was born into the family of Benjamin Franklin Sterling and Mary Jane O'Bryan on August 13, 1866, in Liberty County, Texas. He was

Bryan Sterling Sr. *Courtesy of Betty Sterling Williamson.*

one of twelve children: Samuel Houston, Cora Angelica, Annie Leara, Franklin Pryor, Florence May, John Love, Ross Shaw (who became the governor of Texas in 1930—see Ross Street), Catherine Lavinia, James Bennett (see Sterling Street), Benjamin Garland and Albert Alexander. They were raised in Liberty and Chambers Counties. O.B. worked with his brothers in the founding and formation of the Humble Oil Company.

O.B. lived in the River Oaks area of Houston and, in the early 1900s, returned to Dayton, where he settled in to work and bought property. He was soon to meet his bride-to-be, Lulu Crites. Miss Crites came to Dayton by train seeking a teaching position in the growing community. O.B. saw her as she was getting off the train and told his friends, "I'm going to marry that woman." They were married on January 24, 1912, in Dayton and had five children: Gwendolyn, Lee Franklin, Oliver Bryan Sterling Jr., Mary Lu and Betty Ross.

O.B. invested in land in and around Dayton. One of these properties paralleled what is now known as Sterling Street and Bryan Street. On Sterling Street, he placed several houses as rental properties. On Main Street, he built the Rio Movie Theatre. In the early days of running the theater, O.B. Sr. took note that not many tickets had been sold on one particular afternoon. He checked in the theater to find seating capacity nearly full. He discovered O.B. Jr. selling his own tickets at the back of the entrance of the theater. The Main Street property later sold to Dayton State Bank.

O.B. Bryan Sterling Sr. died in Dayton on April 16, 1946, and was buried in Houston at Glenwood Cemetery. Many of his descendants still reside in Dayton, including grandchildren, great-grandchildren and great-great-grandchildren.[16]

Cherry Creek Road

This street is named for early Texas pioneer John Cherry, who came to Liberty County in 1835, when he was granted a league of land (4,428 acres) by the Mexican government on the west bank of the Trinity River, opposite from his father's league on the east side. Though he didn't live in West Liberty, as Dayton was called at that time, he frequented the area and was well known to most of its inhabitants.

John Cherry was born on November 23, 1808, to Aaron Sr. and Penelope Cherry in Highland County, Ohio. When he was ten years old, John came to Texas in 1819 with his family, which included at least seven siblings. They first settled along the Coushatta Indian village on the Trinity River near what is now Sheperd, Texas. He grew up among the Indians and learned their language, speaking it fluently.

Soon after arriving in Texas, he established himself as a hunter by killing a large panther from a tree with a single-barrel muzzleloading flintlock rifle. After killing the cat, he stripped it of its hide, which was used like money in trade. Taking it home to his father, who often traded with his friend Jean LaFitte of Galveston, Aaron remarked that it was the largest panther pelt he had ever seen in his long and adventurous life.

John Cherry. *Courtesy of the Cherry family.*

The Aaron Cherry family, which included seven children, is listed in the 1826 U.S. Census of the Atascocito District, as all of Southeast Texas was known, with John listed as age nineteen.

John Cherry married his first wife, Matilda C. Bridges, in 1829 under Mexican law and lived in Nacogdoches County. According to an account written by Homer Cherry,[17] John met Sam Houston in Nacogdoches when Sam first came to Texas. That acquaintance and friendship lasted as long as Houston was alive.

On March 6, 1836, four days after the signing of the Declaration of Texas Independence, John joined Captain William M. Logan's company of Liberty Volunteers, which later became a part of the Second Regiment. The company was organized to relieve Colonel Travis at San Antonio, but the soldiers didn't learn of the fall of the Alamo until their arrival at San Felipe. On the march, John became ill with the measles and was left behind while General Sam Houston continued his retreat up the Brazos River to what is now Hempstead. John later rejoined the command, and according to affidavits by his son, Elisha Cherry, and others, he participated in the Battle of San Jacinto.

On the day following the victory, General Houston sent John Cherry on a peace mission to the Indians. The Alabama and Coushatta Indians gave him a warm welcome, but the Cherokee Indians had been stirred up by the Mexicans and were very hostile to the new Texas government. When Cherry approached their chief, he was received with personal goodwill but was warned to "tell old Sam Houston he had better stay away from here."[18] Consequently, Cherry rode all night on the return trip to give this information to General Houston. The final result was the Cherokee War. In 1838, President Sam Houston issued a voucher for seventy-five dollars to John Cherry for his services as an interpreter for the Indians.

In 1882, John was given 1,280 acres of bounty land in Tom Green and Irion Counties. This was promised by the decree of March 21, 1838, to all soldiers who joined the army in the future and remained until the end of the war. In 1878, Cherry applied for and later received an annual pension from the State of Texas as a veteran of the Texas Revolution.

With his first wife, Matilda Bridges (1812–1849), Cherry had seven children, two of whom may have died in infancy. In the 1850 U.S. census of Liberty County, Liberty Township, John, a farmer, is listed as head of the household with seven children living with him; his wife, Matilda, had died in 1849. Some sources say John's second wife was Roxy Line White (1803–1851), but the marriage must not have lasted long, as she also married a man named Merritt.

Cherry married his third wife, Frances Holt Smith (1828–1891), on February 8, 1851, and, about that same time, acquired land in Tarkington Prairie near the present town of Cleveland, Texas, where they built a double log house. All of the Indians in that part of the country were friendly with him and would often seek his counsel. His friend Sam Houston also visited him there. The 1860 census of Tarkington Prairie shows that he and Frances had seven children, one of whom was hers from a previous marriage.

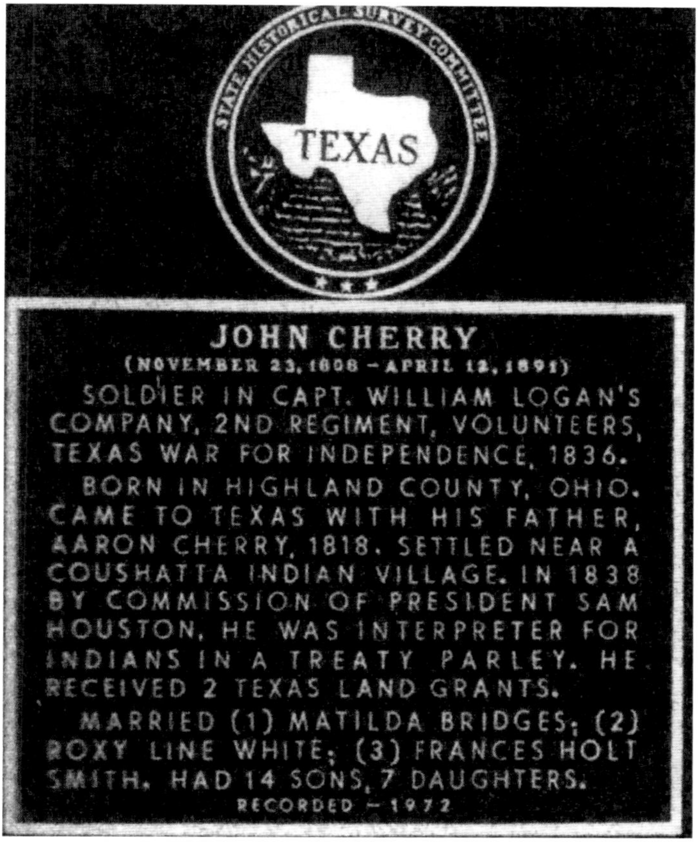

Historical marker at Ryan Cemetery. *Courtesy of the Texas State Historical Commission.*

At one time, Cherry was considered moderately wealthy, possessing large tracts of land, many slaves, large herds of cattle and a nice sum of money. However, the Civil War freed his slaves and made his money counterfeit. But his slaves remained with him and took his name, and he only lost their sale value. Still, the hardships of Reconstruction days left him reduced to a poor man.

The 1870 census of Tarkington Prairie lists John, Frances and eleven children living there. Cherry later accumulated some money that he stored away in auger holes in the logs of his house. He became much involved in horse racing, owning a race track and fine horses that won many races, but he finally lost heavily and the loss was more than he could stand in his old age.

The 1880 census lists ten children living with John, now seventy-one, and Frances, forty-seven. John joined the Baptist Church when he was more than eighty years old and was baptized by Reverend J.A. Lea in a pool on his own land in Tarkington Prairie one cold January day in 1890. He died on April 12, 1891, and is buried in the Ryan Cemetery at Tarkington Prairie near his home. Frances also died in 1891 and is buried beside him. A state historical marker placed in 1972 marks the site of their graves.

Chester Street

Chester Street is named after Aaron Chester Holbrook Sr. and is located in the Holbrook subdivision, a seventy-four-acre tract of land bounded by North Winfree Street, East Lawrence Street and Cherry Creek Road. Known as Chester, he developed the subdivision in 1962,[19] naming two of the roads for his sisters, Evelyn and Juanita; one after his friend Morgan Laird; one for the Holbrook family; and two for himself, using his first and middle names. (See the Aaron Street and Holbrook Street sections.)

Chester was a pioneer in modern road construction methods, building the first sand/shell base for an asphalt road, State Highway 146, to Mont Belvieu from Dayton with his partner, Will Graves. He had a varied career as a rice farmer, contractor and builder, business owner and subdivision developer.

He also had a reputation as a great practical joker. In an article for the *Liberty Vindicator* in 1982, he said, "I was always pulling jokes on somebody. Still do every time I get a chance."

In addition to pulling pranks, Chester loved flying airplanes, purchasing his first when flying was in its infancy. His planes were used for both business and pleasure. When he was doing contracting work, he would fly to Austin for bid openings. Among other places, he flew to San Francisco, Canada, Mexico City and Alaska. He once landed in the Aleutian Islands.

Chester Holbrook. *Courtesy of the* Liberty Vindicator.

He went everywhere without mapping out a route. Flying was an adventure in those days, and he laughed as he related some of his experiences in the 1982 article. On the way home to Dayton from Alaska, he recalled that he was flying above the clouds when he decided to come down and see where he was. He had already flown half-way across the Gulf of Mexico and had to turn around and go back about two hundred miles. He recalled one time when he offered a visiting New Yorker a lift in his plane. He and the New Yorker had to walk all over the landing field kicking down ant hills before they could take off.[20]

Chester Holbrook passed away on February 21, 1990.[21] His wife, Ellen (Nelson), had died in 1987.[22] They are buried at Magnolia Park Cemetery in Dayton.

Church Street

Church Street was originally named First Street, as shown on the 1927 map of Dayton.[23] The first indication of a name change was in the Dayton City Council minutes of October 10, 1929, when Church Street is mentioned. The exact date of the name change is not known. The street was so named because two early Dayton churches were located on the street: Dayton Baptist Church, later known as the First Baptist Church, and Methodist Episcopal Church, later known as the First United Methodist Church.

In the early days, both churches met in schoolhouses—the Baptists in a one-room school located on what is today East Cook Street and the Methodists in a building believed to be a schoolhouse located near Linney Cemetery. These early churches did not have full-time pastors who lived in the town but rather had traveling pastors, called circuit riders, who visited many towns preaching the Gospel, sometimes to all denominations at once.

The Baptist Church was organized in 1878: "In obedience to Christ's commission, and under the leadership of the Holy Spirit, ten Christians met in 1878 in the tiny town of Dayton, Texas, and formed the Baptist Church."[24] The congregation met in the schoolhouse until 1895, when several circuit rider preachers who held services for the Dayton church—those listed in the church minutes were Missionary H.W. Pickett, J.H.H. Ellis and Brother W.S. Hogue—encouraged the church to move from the school to a different location. A member of the congregation recalled, "After preaching they & the church and congregation had a considerable contention whether the meeting should be continued at the school house or be moved to Wilson's Church which was decided in favor of the Church."[25]

Wilson's Church, also called Union Church because several denominations met in the building, was located on the southeast corner of present-day Waring and North Main Streets. A written history confirming this fact about the church stated, "By this time there was other denomations [*sic*] here so they all went togather [*sic*] and built a Union Church, across the St from wher[e] Mrs. Uncle lives now."[26]

Minutes of the Southeast Texas Baptist Association give the only information on Wilson's Church: "Charles Wilson was a prominent Methodist layman who passed away before I came to Dayton in 1917. I think he was a lawyer. He owned a lot of property in Dayton, and lived across the street from the Community Church. It was also called the Union Church, and possibly Wilson's Church. He may have given the land where the church was built."[27]

During a church conference following preaching by J.F. McLeod on December 12, 1897, the minutes showed that the Baptist Church was then called the Dayton Baptist Church of Christ. The church continued to use that name until 1911, when the church minutes recorded the name as the Dayton Baptist Church.

The Union Church (or Wilson's Church) continued to be the meeting place for the Baptist church until "in 1900 a storm damaged the building so much that it was not safe to meet in any more. So, the Baptists moved to a building noun [*sic*] as Clompton's [Compton's] Store. This building was on the corner wher[e] Mr. Ulmer had his last store."[28]

The 1900 storm mentioned was the hurricane that destroyed Galveston Island on September 8. Because of this storm, the church not only met in Compton's store (located on what is now the southwest corner of Winfree and U.S. Highway 90) but also in church members' homes and other buildings until the latter part of 1901, when the church bought the land north of the present sanctuary site, one block south of U.S. Highway 90 on South Church Street.

The main event for the Baptists in 1901 was the construction of the new church building. A written history by a church member at that time recorded, "Brother McCloud [McLeod] gave a lot to build on. The lumber was hauled from S. Hicks S.M. [Sawmill] 5 m. The men gave the[i]r labor and we had a new ch—Mrs. Anderson gave a bell."[29]

The land records from the Liberty County Courthouse showed the purchase of the land to build the new church was made by J.F. McLeod, pastor in 1898, and W.C. Moore for $1,000 from Charles Wilson on December 15, 1897. The church trustees—C.H. Simmons, W.S. Lowery

Dayton Baptist Church of Christ, 1901. *Courtesy of First Baptist Church.*

and Mrs. Nora Spears—purchased the land from these two men for $1.00 on July 27, 1901.

After having been established as a church for twenty-three years, the congregation finally had a permanent Baptist church building. This was the first denominational church building erected in Dayton.

The name First Baptist Church was recorded in the church minutes for the first time on August 7, 1929. In 1934, Mrs. Emil Joseph Stoesser gave the church one lot of land that bordered the existing buildings, and the church was remodeled and enlarged to include a two-story brick Sunday school annex, housing a large assembly room, classrooms and a kitchen on the first floor, with another assembly room and classrooms on the second floor, and a brick-veneer five-thousand-square-foot auditorium with new baptistry, a church office and several classrooms. The dedication for these new facilities was in November 1934.

In 1954, the church erected a new sanctuary and educational building. In 1981, in conjunction with the church's 103rd anniversary celebration, a dedication took place for the present Family Life Center, which included a gymnasium, a running track, a den, a kitchen, Sunday school rooms,

First Baptist Church, 1934. *Courtesy of First Baptist Church.*

First Baptist Church, 1954. *Courtesy of First Baptist Church.*

restrooms and offices.[30] As of this writing, the First Baptist Church is still housed in these facilities on Church Street.

The first valid record of a Methodist Church in Dayton was recorded in the Methodist Houston District minutes where early pastor appointments were made. An appointment appears to a mission in "West Liberty," as Dayton was known until the 1880s, in 1863.[31] According to a news item appearing in the *Liberty Vindicator* on Friday, March 3, 1893, "There is no church house, but church is held once a month in the school house."

"Dayton Mission" is first mentioned in 1898 in

the Houston District records of the Methodist Conference. By 1908, the church was known as a station church, referring perhaps to the fact that Dayton was a station on the Texas and New Orleans Railroad in the 1870s. The Methodists later had services in the Union Church building located on North Main Street near the site of the R.N. Ford home.[32]

In 1901, deed records in the Liberty County Court House show that:

> *Mr. B.F. Cameron sold to trustees of the Methodist Church Episcopal South at Dayton, Texas for ten dollars several lots to be used, kept, maintained, and disposed of as a place of Divine worship for the use of the ministry and membership of the Methodist Episcopal Church, South, subject to the discipline, usage and appointments of said church, as from time to time authorized and declared by the general conference of said church and by the Annual Conference within whose bounds the said premises are situated.*

The first house of worship was erected in 1906 on the corner of Highway 90 and Church Street, just across the street from the building known as Bozeman's or Young's, which is now occupied by the Boot Barn. This remained a circuit church until 1908, when it became a station charge under the leadership of Reverend T.B. Whitten. This same year, the church in Dayton became a church in its own right and an annex was added to the church to be used primarily to care for the youth and children and facilitate proper room for their activities. The Sunday school was organized in 1906, with Mr. Charles Wilson elected the first superintendent.[33]

In 1924, the church board saw a real need for larger and better-equipped facilities for the growing church and its many activities and began purchasing land to move the church from its Church Street location. At the new site on the corner of Houston Avenue and Cleveland Street, a brick structure was completed in 1928. The cornerstone listed Reverend A.W. Gordon as pastor and the building committee as J.T. Tadlock, W.T. Jamison, J.B. Sterling, T.H. Shaw, M.W. Ford and A.W. Runyan. This building served well for almost half a century.

An educational/children's building was completed and consecrated in September 1959. Bishop Frank Smith presided, with the assistance from District Superintendent Clenden. The pastor at the time was Reverend James Calloway. The building was used for classrooms, a nursery, the pastor's study, a secretary's office and the Mother's Day Out program.

In 1967, plans were made to build an addition to the church: a fellowship-youth building. The Service of Consecration was held during the morning

Left: Methodist Episcopal Church, 1906. *Courtesy of First United Methodist Church.*

Below: First United Methodist Church, 1928. *Courtesy of First United Methodist Church.*

worship service on January 14, 1968, with Bishop Paul E. Martin presiding, assisted by Dr. Ed M. Mathinson, district superintendent. The pastor was Reverend Robert B. Lowe.

Progress and time took their tolls, and it was determined that there was a need for a new church sanctuary. The 1924 cornerstone was removed in 1980, when the building was demolished in preparation for the new sanctuary. On January 6, 1980, the congregation of the United Methodist

First United Methodist Church, 1981. *Courtesy of First United Methodist Church.*

Clarence Dearbonne Sr. *Courtesy of Lena Ruth Dearbonne Allen.*

Church gathered and ground was broken to build a new four-hundred-seat sanctuary. This building project occurred during the pastorate of Reverend William C. Webb Jr. A consecration service was held on Sunday, July 28, 1981.[34]

The First United Methodist Church remains located at the corner of Houston and Cleveland Streets.

Clarence Street

Clarence Street is named for Clarence Dearbonne Sr., who was born on November 30, 1901, in Mallet, Louisiana, to Noah and Lena Dearbonne. Clarence grew up with eight siblings: Anderson, James, Preston, Murphey, Anthony, Robert, Elvina Dearbonne La Chapelle and Bertha Dearbonne Goudeau. He attended school in Opelausas, Louisiana, which was close to Mallet.

Clarence moved to Anahuac, Texas, at some point and then to Dayton in the early 1940s in search of employment. He married Alice Baldwin, a seamstress, of Liberty, Texas, in the late 1940s. The couple had no children, but Clarence had two children from a previous marriage: Clarence Dearbonne Jr. and Lena Ruth Dearbonne Allen.

Clarence was a great cook who worked at a number of cafés and restaurants in the area and eventually opened his own café called the Snuggle Inn, located in the Lowe Woods community of Dayton on Colbert Street. He specialized in barbecue, tamales, gumbo and sausage links. He catered banquets for the American Rice Growers Association and cooked for a group of deer hunters, of which he was a part, for years. He also owned rental properties.

Clarence organized and owned a local men's baseball team called the Dayton Tigers. For years, they played other teams, providing big entertainment for the community. He frequently went to wrestling matches in Houston on Friday nights, and if he didn't go to a wrestling match in person, he watched one on TV. His daughter, Lena Ruth, remembers one night when her dad decided to clean his gun while watching the match. "As deer hunting season was approaching, he thought that would be the perfect time to spruce up his hunting rifle. He didn't know that a bullet was in the chamber. All of a sudden, BANG! That was the night his favorite wrestler, Bull Curry, was defeated. Dad was never able to live it down. Everyone laughed and said he was trying to shoot Bull Curry's opponent. Some folks still laugh about that to this day."

Clarence Dearbonne died of a stroke on September 17, 1965, and is buried in Wells Cemetery at Liberty, Texas.[35]

Clayton Street

Clayton Street had two previous names. It was first called Alden[36] and later called Liberty Avenue.[37] It was renamed for Clayton Leo Moreau, born on February 10, 1919, who was the son of Leo and Maedee Moreau. He was born and raised in Dayton and contracted polio at a young age. He had one brother, Wilmer M. "Bill" Moreau.

This article appeared in the *Dayton News* in February 1942:

> *Clayton Moreau, son of Mr. and Mrs. Leo Moreau, whose 24th birthday was on the 10th, celebrated the event Sunday, the 14th with a birthday dinner. Only relatives and a few friends numbering 27, were present to enjoy the occasion.*
>
> *Clayton, being crippled, can't fight with guns and bayonets, but is doing his best to help with the war. Practically one hundred percent of his allowance from his parents is put into defense bonds. An extra incentive*

Clayton Moreau. *Courtesy of Punky Moreau Shanks.*

in wanting to help with the war is the fact that his younger brother, Wilmer, is in the service, and by this time probably overseas. Besides wearing apparel and other gifts Sunday, Clayton received enough money to buy another defense bond.[38]

Clayton loved baseball and football and his favorite team was Texas A&M. As an older man, he was often seen sitting on his front porch watching traffic drive by. He passed away on October 1, 1970, at the age of fifty-one.[39]

Cleveland Street and State Highway 321

The stretch of road called Cleveland was named as such because it runs from the city of Dayton to the city of Cleveland and has three different designated names, depending on its location.

South Cleveland Street runs south from U.S. Highway 90 until it dead ends at Lovers Lane. North Cleveland Street runs north from U.S. Highway 90, passing through residential Dayton as a four-lane highway before narrowing down to a two-lane state highway. State Highway 321 officially begins at the same designation as North Cleveland Street, but locals begin to refer to it as such at the two-lane point. It's also called the Cleveland Highway.

South Cleveland Street has been an important and well-traveled street for many years because of the construction of several schools, two churches, the original public library building and a city complex that includes the present public library and community center. The portion of the street that existed in 1936 was paved that year, according to Alphene Richter, wife of Dr. E.R. Richter, longtime residents of Dayton. She said, "It was a dirt road when we moved here in 1936. The city began paving it that year."[40]

A large two-story brick school called the Dayton School began construction in 1909 and housed elementary through high school students. It was built facing U.S. Highway 90, with South Cleveland Street as its boundary to the west. It became the junior high and elementary school when a new high school was built farther south on South Cleveland in 1951. The two-story school was demolished following the construction of a newer high school, located on State Highway 146, in 1975.

Another school, Stephen F. Austin Elementary, was built even farther south on the street in 1962. Linda Blackburn Harris recalls that on the first day of the new school (which opened in the middle of the school year), all the students walked in a line down the street to the new building carrying their books from the old two-story school.[41]

Two churches make their homes on South Cleveland Street. The First United Methodist Church relocated from Church Street (see the Church Street section) and erected a new house of worship on South Cleveland in 1928, directly west of the Dayton School. This church building was replaced in 1981 with the present sanctuary.

St. Joseph's the Worker Catholic Church relocated to its present location on South Cleveland in 1984 from its location north of Dayton on Highway 321. First built was the Catholic Hall facility, where the congregation met until 1984, when the sanctuary and parsonage was built.

Two other important buildings are located on the street. The Edmund E. and Nida Smith Jones Public Library was erected in 1984, with Cleveland Street as its east boundary. When voters decided they needed a larger library and also a community center, the two were combined in a lovely facility farther south on the street, across from the Catholic church. This new library opened in 2009. The previous library building was purchased by Dayton Independent School District and is now the Educational Support Center.

Interestingly, the Dayton City Council minutes of May 31, 1961, revealed that the newly hired city attorney, Harlan Friend, informed the council that the City of Liberty still owned South Cleveland Street and the streets in the South Town League (Waco Street and South Clayton). He discovered this while drawing up an assessment ordinance (for the paving of South Cleveland Street). He reported to the council on June 5, 1961, that he had started the proper procedures for drawing up a quick claim deed to give the streets to Dayton.

With the construction of Stephen F. Austin Elementary School, the city endeavored to extend the paving of South Cleveland down to the school. The council decided to assess the property owners of that portion of the street to help with the paving. Those property owners were T.H. Wallace, Lloyd Gano, Kenneth Canion Sr., J.B. Jamison, Ben Entsminger and R.V.

Young. The council also assessed Dayton ISD. A special council meeting was held on June 26, 1961, to allow the property owners to express their views or contest the levy of $4.00 per linear foot assessed for the paving. A lively discussion ensued. At the July 14, 1961 city council meeting, it was decided to charge the property owners $3.00 per foot for the paving. A.C. Construction Company of Houston (the low bidder) was hired to do the paving at a cost of $27,028.

The paving proceeded, and at the September 5, 1961 city council meeting, the mayor and council discussed the new pavement, which was already cracking. At a later meeting, Marvin Henry informed the council that the reason for the cracked pavement on South Cleveland could not be pinpointed; therefore, they could not hold the contractor responsible, but the contractor had agreed to chip out the cracked parts and fill it with OA 59, an asphalt material. That seems to be the end of the paving project.

North Cleveland Street: Immediately north of U.S. Highway 90, the Union Pacific Railroad crosses North Cleveland. The Dayton City Council formed a committee in the late 1980s to investigate the possibility of building of an overpass or underpass for the railroad, as the town came to a complete standstill when a train passed through town or when a train stopped on the tracks, as they so often did. State highway funds were obtained, and an underpass was completed in July 1990.

State Highway 321 is called the "Cleveland Highway" by locals and officially begins at the intersection of U.S. Highway 90 in Dayton running north and ends at Loop 573 in Cleveland, about twenty-two miles. It's part of the eastern Greater Houston area evacuation route, providing a corridor for the communities of Baytown, Kemah and Pasadena. According to the *Handbook of Texas*, State Highway 321 is believed to cover part of the Nacogdoches Lynchberg Trail.

Local longtime resident Jack Unkel said that before the Cleveland Highway was paved, if it rained, you had to get to Cleveland by horse.[42]

Records with the Texas Department of Transportation's Liberty office show that this road was named a state highway between December 1939 and August 1942. It was paved in 1935 from Dayton to 1.3 miles north of Luce Bayou, and the entire stretch was completed probably in 1942.[43]

Colbert Street

Annie Colbert. *Courtesy of the Rosenwald School Museum.*

Colbert Street was originally called Balsam.[44] It was later renamed for Annie E. Colbert, born on February 5, 1866, who was hired in 1892 from the Houston area to teach African American students in Dayton. W.F. Blair, who owned and operated one of the best-known early sawmills at Dayton as early as 1891, also operated a school for the mill employees' children and boarded schoolteacher Annie Colbert in his home.[45]

In the 1900 Liberty County census, schedule 1, W.F. Blair was enumerated at Precinct 4, residence 246, as "owner of sawmill," and one can discern that about twenty persons living adjacent to his home were probably employees of his mill. These included Phil Green, J.L. Hodges, Ben Brantley, Drury Jackson, W.J. Alexander, Wesley Edge, John Spraker, Andrew Spraker, Thomas Colbert, Albert Dillenbeck, Huey Alexander and others. According to Dayton ISD, Mrs. Colbert was in Dayton from 1892 to 1914.

One of Annie's first chores was to construct a building where she could hold classes, and her older students were recruited to assist her. That building was eventually demolished. Another school building, part of the present school on Colbert Street, was built in 1933, constructed years after Mrs. Colbert's departure from Dayton.[46]

This building, partly funded by the Rosenwald Foundation, was originally named the Dayton Colored School. In 1935, the building was renamed the Annie E. Colbert School. Dayton ISD received a restoration grant in 2010 from the Lowe's Charitable and Educational Foundation in partnership with the National Trust for Historic Preservation. A portion of the school was torn down, keeping and restoring the original Rosenwald School, which is now used as a museum for the campus and community, as well as for community events. It was dedicated in 2010.[47] Colbert Street runs in front of the school and continues north across U.S. Highway 90.

Mr. Wilbert Wycliff, who graduated from the school in 1935 and was ninety-two years old in 2010, got the honor as a teenager of chauffeuring Mrs. Colbert from her home in Houston to Dayton for the renaming ceremony. Annie Colbert died on June 10, 1961.

Coleman Street

Coleman Street was originally called Coplay[48] and was renamed after Oscar Howard Coleman and his wife, Nancy Evelyn Norcross. The couple made their home on that street and lived there until their deaths in the 1950s. Oscar was born on November 11, 1878, to John Alexander and Mary Jane Stephens Coleman in Tunis, Burleson County, Texas. He had at least one sister, listed in his obituary as Mrs. Frank Barclay, and a brother, Nels Coleman.

Nancy, who went by her middle name of Evelyn, was born on August 2, 1881, probably also in Burleson County, Texas, based on the fact that her mother died there in 1889 when Evelyn was eight years old. She was the daughter of George Washington and Mary Emeline Shaver Norcross and was reared with nine siblings.

The date and place of their marriage is not known, but it most likely took place in Burleson County, where they had both lived as children. By the time of the 1910 U.S. census, the Colemans were living in Beaumont, Texas. They moved to Dayton prior to 1917, when Oscar's World War I draft registration card was issued in Liberty County during 1917–18. As evidenced in the 1920 census, the Colemans had four children: Mary Lee Coleman Colbert, Ruby Gene Coleman Huddleston, Georgia Bertie Coleman McGinnis and Oscar Alexander.

Evelyn (referred to as Mrs. O.H. Coleman) was listed in Dayton ISD's 1920 school yearbook, *The Sheaf*, as a member of the parent-teacher association.

Oscar's occupation was rice farmer, presumably with his brother, Nels, who was also a rice farmer who resided in Dayton.

Coleman Street was known as "Silk Stocking Lane," according to Rose Klimitchek, whose family moved to the street in the 1950s. It was so called because several prominent women lived on the street: Mrs. Coleman, Mrs. W.T. Jamison and Mrs. T.O. Johnson, to name a few.[49]

The Colemans attended the First United Methodist Church, and their memorial services were held there. Evelyn passed away on December 5, 1956, at age sventy-five,[50] and Oscar died on April 15, 1959, at age eighty.[51] Both are buried at Linney Cemetery in Dayton.

Collins Street

Tom Collins. *Courtesy of Iris Collins Eaton.*

Collins Street is named for Thomas "Tom" Vaught Collins, son of Thomas Edgar and Lura Bell McDonald Dunaway Collins. Tom, who has traced his family line to President James Madison, a cousin, was born on August 2, 1907, in Darbun, Walthall County, Mississippi, and grew up nearby in Foxworth with six siblings: Rich, Robert, Rose, Connie, Gladys and Edna. After high school graduation, he attended the mechanical school in St. Louis. His older brother was attending school there, and Tom begged his parents to let him go with him. Throughout his life, Tom had a knack for being able to fix almost anything.

Tom came to Dayton in 1929 to work at his uncle's Cadillac dealership. He met Louise Catherine Stoesser, and they were married in October 1936. Louise, a homemaker, raised their four children: Iris Collins Eaton, Gary Roy, Thomas Edward (Tommy) and John Richard. Tom had another child by a previous marriage named Thomas T. Vaught. Louise was also an excellent manager of the rental properties she and Tom owned when they were young. After Tom passed away, she purchased more rental properties and managed her own real estate company to support the family.

Tom was a successful entrepreneur who did well in his pursuits. He had a restaurant called the Tom Collins Café on Highway 90, where he got to know many families in the oil business as they traveled between Houston and Liberty. Tom also had a talent for investing money well. Before World War II, he invested in duplexes and triple apartments along Alan Parkway in Houston, which he sold after the war at a great profit. He sold insurance before opening his own insurance company in 1955 called Production National Life Insurance Company. For many years, he was a member of the Million Dollar Round Table, an association for insurance agents exhibiting superior performance. Collins also sold lots for homes on South Main and Church Streets, building several himself.

Tom was one of the founders of the Dayton Volunteer Fire Department and was elected the first fire chief. During the years 1944–48, he was mayor of Dayton, and it was his goal to get streets paved. He successfully showed the city council how to float a bond election, and they were able to pave streets and install streetlights. Tom was also instrumental in getting the Dayton Hospital built. Retired Texas governor Ross Sterling owned property on North Winfree, and Tom prevailed on him to sell or donate it to the city so that a hospital could be built. Sterling agreed, saying, "No one ever asked me before." Tom and Louise made a contribution that paid for the X-ray equipment for the hospital.

Tom Collins is described by his daughter Iris as being kind and loving, inspiring to people and brilliant in math. He helped needy people by showing them how to get mortgages for homes and how to manage their money. He taught his children how to invest money wisely. Iris described him as a very nurturing parent who loved to have fun. He loved telling jokes and pulling practical jokes as well.[52] Tom's son John, remembers that when his dad started his fire insurance company in 1958, half of all the properties in Dayton bought policies. His dad auctioned off a few shares in the company and donated that money to cover the cost of fire insurance policies for Dayton's churches for one year. When John was in elementary school, his dad won the contract for insuring students against personal injury. Kids brought money to school if their parents wanted them to have the coverage. The parents would send a dollar or two for the special coverage, and his dad collected a box full of money from the teacher of each class.[53]

Tom died in 1962 at the age of fifty-five. His wife, Louise, died in 1986. They are buried in Magnolia Park Cemetery in Dayton.

Daisy Street

Daisy Street was named for Daisy Flowers, wife of James Sidney Flowers Sr. and mother of James S. Flowers Jr. She was born on December 18, 1882, at Chadmore, England, near Cannock, South Staffordshire. She came to the United States through Canada with her family around 1900. Her family stayed in Canada long enough to make "travel money" to Texas and then settled in La Costa around 1902 because her father had family there who worked for the railroad. Her dad also hired on with the railroad and was transferred to San Antonio. Daisy met James Sidney Flowers on September 28, 1902, and the two were married on April 12, 1903, at her home. James was born on February 23, 1875, in Woodville, Texas.

Daisy moved with her new husband to Nome, Texas, where they lived in railroad cars on the sidetracks. The Flowers' moved to Dayton soon thereafter, with James first employed by the Southern Pacific Railroad, though later he became Dayton's constable. The "section house" that belonged to the railroad was their home until they built their own house in 1909 at 804 North Cleveland Street, where it stands as of this writing. They resided there for sixty years. The couple had four children, two sons and two daughters. The oldest son and the girls died young, but James S. Flowers Jr. lived with his mother and father until he married.

Daisy Flowers. *Courtesy of Lillie Flowers.*

Like her husband, Daisy was very active in the community. She was a faithful member of the Methodist Church and a Sunday school teacher for about fifty years. She was one of the organizers of the popular "Egg Circle" in 1906 and was a charter member of the Priscilla Club in 1910. As a Priscilla, she spent many hours crocheting, tatting and making baskets for the county fair each year and, during World War I, helped form a Red Cross Auxiliary, the members of which made comfort kits, sweaters and socks for the soldiers. She and the other Priscillas folded bandages and did work to assist the Red Cross during World War II.

Daisy also helped charter the Dayton Garden Club in 1932 and was a charter member of Eastern Star. She enjoyed oil painting, playing the piano and loved sewing and doing fancy needlework. For many Christmases, she could be found around town delivering boxes of homemade candy and bags of fruit. Later in life, Daisy loved to read to and play the piano for her little granddaughter Lisa.

Daisy died on October 17, 1967, at the Dayton Memorial Hospital and is buried at Magnolia Park Cemetery in Dayton.[54]

Dale Street

This street was named by Harry Charles Brown in honor of his grandson, Norman Dale Brown Jr. (called Dale). Dale was born in Houston on June 2, 1958, to Norman Dale and Martha Hale Brown. He and his siblings—Nancy, Jo and Susan—have lived in Dayton most of their lives, except for three exciting years. In 1970, Dale's dad was transferred to Holland to supervise a chemical plant for Gulf Oil Company, and of course, the family went with him. Dale's fondest memories of Holland are from when he was twelve and the family was living by the coast, where they could walk to the beach, and of the beautiful flowers in the spring. The subsequent two years, the family lived in South Korea, again following Norman's job. Dale went to high school at an American military base and had a teacher who sponsored a traveling culture club. One weekend each month, the class took a trip somewhere within the country so that the students, about thirty of them, could learn about and appreciate the Korean country and people.

Dale Brown. *Courtesy of Jo Brown Riley.*

Dale's family returned to Dayton when he was a sophomore in high school, and he became a member of the Dayton High School band, playing percussion.

A year later, a cute little freshman girl named Michelle Boyer caught his eye, and they had their first date on September 13, 1975. Asked how in the world he could remember that date, he replied, "Well, September 13 is also the date we became engaged, and it's my mother's birthday." They dated on and off until they married in May 1979, and they eventually had two children, Joshua and Jessica.

Dale graduated from Dayton High School in 1976 and attended Texas A&M for two years. He elected to leave college when he got a job at Exxon Mobil in 1978 and, as of this writing, has completed thirty-three years at that company.

Dale served as a member of the TVE Committee, a charitable organization that exists to benefit the youth of Liberty and Chambers Counties with scholarships generated by a fair and rodeo, and served for twelve years as a trustee on the Dayton Independent School District School Board. He was elected to the Dayton City Council in May 2013.[55]

Depot Street

Depot Street had two previous names. It was first called Railroad Avenue[56] and later called Commerce Street.[57] It came into being when Dayton (known then as West Liberty, but also variously called Days Station and Dayton Station) became a flag stop for the Texas and New Orleans Railroad, work on the tracks completed there in 1860.[58]

Being a railroad stop, Dayton's population grew, as did its industries: primarily lumbering, rice farming and oil production, which now had access to the trains to transport their products. The railroad also took on passengers, carrying them to Houston, Liberty and Beaumont.[59]

Depot Street became a lively area where businesses sprang up across the tracks from the depot building. By 1908, these businesses included the Original Jones Saloon, William Bolton's Store, the Shroeder Saloon and Salle's Drug Store. Old photos reveal an unidentified hotel and another drugstore, as well as other unidentified businesses.

In 1913, a fire began in the Original Jones Saloon that completely destroyed it and damaged surrounding buildings, most of which were wooden structures. There being no fire department, a bucket brigade formed

Dayton was a fuel stop on the Texas and New Orleans Railroad, later merging into the Southern Pacific system. *Courtesy of* Texas Illustrated Magazine.

Train depot on the right with the Original Jones Saloon and other businesses on the left in 1908. *Courtesy of* Texas Illustrated Magazine.

to fight the blaze. Residents pulled mattresses, furniture and merchandise from the spreading fire. Folks said the saloon experienced only an eighteen-hour pause in business and reopened in new quarters the next day.[60]

The train depot building fell into disuse in the 1970s, and as it was being torn down in 1986, Dayton Historical Society founder Mary Beth Jamison,was able to get mementos in the form of square nails and roofing tiles. These are on display at Dayton's Old School Museum.

Edgar Street

Edgar Street was named after Robert B. Edgar, a sawmill man who worked for the Dayton Lumber Company back in the early 1900s.

The 1880 U.S. census revealed that Edgar was born in Michigan in 1874 to Robert Edgar, who was born in Ireland, and Mary J. Edgar, who was born in Pennsylvania. He had four siblings.[61]

R.B. Edgar, 1920. *Courtesy of* The Sheaf *(1920 yearbook of Dayton High School).*

The *Southern Industrial and Lumber Review* of January 1909 stated, "Mr. R.B. Edgar is the sales manager and treasurer of The Dayton Lumber Company. He looks after the handling of orders sent in through the sales office of the Alfred Bennett Lumber Company at St. Louis which organized the Dayton Co. in 1905."[62]

The next census where he could be found was in 1910, when he was listed living in Dayton with his wife, Lottie Martin Edgar, who was born in 1885 in Tennessee, and their son Robert, who was born in Arkansas in 1906.

In a book including several pages about the Dayton Lumber Company, Edgar was mentioned as the sales agent, one of the key personnel members, for the company when it reorganized as the Dayton Mills Company in 1915. He worked with mill owner Ross Sterling (see Ross Street), A.E. Kerr (see Kerr Street) and E.P. Ladd (see Ladd Street).[63]

In the 1920 census, the Edgars still lived in Dayton and had added children to the growing family: Mary E., Doris and Charlotte. R.B. and Lottie were active in the school system. R.B. served on the Dayton ISD school board and is pictured in the 1920 yearbook, *The Sheaf*. Lottie Edgar was listed as a member of the parent-teacher association.

In another publication, R.B. is listed as a trustee for the Linney Cemetery Association. He signed a deed on June 10, 1922, for ownership of the land for the cemetery.[64]

Sometime in the 1920s, the Dayton Mills Company was sold and dismantled, all of its hardwood timber being depleted.

No information could be found as to when the Edgar family left Dayton, but the 1930 census has them living in Fordyce, Dallas County, Arkansas. R.B. and Lottie had two more children, John and Gene, bringing the total to six. Robert B. Edgar died in 1943. Lottie died in 1961, and both are buried at Oakland Cemetery in Fordyce, Arkansas.

Elaine Street

Elaine Street is named for Elaine Watel Friedman, born on November 25, 1921, in Dallas, Texas, to Hyman and Rose Watel. She grew up in Dallas and graduated from high school there in 1939.

While attending the University of Texas (UT) as a college freshman, she met the love of her life, Saul Friedman. Saul said she was (and still is) a very beautiful woman. Elaine was elected into the Bluebonnet Belles of UT as one of the fifty most beautiful girls at the college. Elaine and Saul were married on January 27, 1940, and moved to Dayton the same year.

Saul Friedman was born in Dayton and lived there until the fourth grade, when his family moved to Houston. He graduated from San Jacinto High School in Houston and then from the University of Texas in 1940, where he received both his law and business degrees in five years. He was quite active while there, serving as assistant manager of the football team, pitcher on the intramural baseball team and president of the Phi Sigma Delta fraternity.

Saul's father owned businesses in Dayton and offered him a salary about eight times what he was being paid to apprentice attorneys. Saul decided

Elaine Friedman. *Courtesy of Saul Friedman.*

to accept his father's offer when he was offered one month's salary in advance. He became a merchant and builder in Dayton while Elaine was a homemaker, raising their two children, Stephen and Susan. Alice Augustine from New Orleans worked for many years for the family as a cook and helped to raise their children.

Saul became active in civic organizations, serving on the Dayton City Council (was mayor pro-tem) and as president of the Dayton Rotary Club. The Friedman family owned much property in Dayton that they subdivided and sold as home sites. Saul named Elaine Street for his wife, another for his daughter, Susan (see Susan Street), and another for his sister, Esther Friendman Blonstein (see Esther Street). The Friedmans moved to Houston in 1956.

As of this writing, the Friedmans have been married for more than seventy years. When asked the secret to such a long marriage, Saul said that he credited their longevity to his mother-in-law, who was an inventor. "She invented brain washing. She would put her finger in front of my nose and tell me, 'You have married a wonderful girl!' over and over." Saul said, "She was correct."[65]

Emma Street

Emma Street is named for Emma Dunn Harris, who was born in Osage City, Kansas, on January 20, 1890, to Irish immigrants Patrick Michael and Anna Keilly Dunn. Emma was the youngest of eleven children.

Emma married Joseph Denton Harris Jr. on December 30, 1920, in Kansas City, Missouri. The couple moved to Bay City, Texas, in 1921 and then to Houston in January of 1923 before settling in Dayton in April 1924 with their two-year-old son, Bobby.

The Harris family lived for a short while in the old Hunnicutt Hotel (see Hunnicutt Street) until they moved into the Edgar House (see Edgar Street) on present North Main Street. Emma raised three children in Dayton—Robert, known as Bobby; Joe; and Jean—while her husband worked initially for the Dayton/Goose Creek Railroad owned by Ross Sterling and then for the TV&N Railroad and Dayton Lumber Company, also owned by Sterling and his partners. After its reorganization in 1912, the Dayton Lumber Company became the Dayton Mills Company and was sold by Sterling in 1920. After another change in ownership and name, it was bought in 1929 by Joe and Emma, who also operated it, eventually renaming it People's Lumber and Supply Company.[66]

The Harrises were members of Immaculate Conception Catholic Church in Liberty and later joined St. Joseph's in Dayton. Emma was interested in civic affairs and actively supported women's rights. She was a member of Dayton's Egg Circle and the Priscilla Club. Her grandson Larry recalled that his grandmother was a feisty, determined woman. She taught her son Bobby, Larry's dad, to read when he was four years old so that he could read to his younger brother, Joe. When Emma dropped her son Joe off at Texas A&M, her parting words were, "Remember the Alamo!" Larry remembers his siblings gathering at his grandparents' house after church on Sundays for snacks and Cokes.[67]

Emma Harris. *Courtesy of Bobby Harris.*

Emma Harris was a proud mother when her son Bobby became the city of Dayton's mayor from 1948 to 1950. Her husband, Joe, then served as mayor from 1952 to 1956. She would have been equally proud to have known that her grandson Larry was mayor from 1991 to 2005, the longest tenure of any mayor.

Emma died in 1977, preceding her husband, who passed away in 1979. Both are buried at Magnolia Park Cemetery in Dayton.

Entzminger Street

Entzminger Street is named for Ben and Jessie Baker Entzminger and runs through the property that they owned. Ben was born on June 9, 1866, in Bronson, Kansas, to George and Saloe Entzminger, who moved to Liberty County in 1904. Ben had thirteen siblings. Jessie was born in Beaumont, Texas, on November 24, 1890, to Thomas B. and LaPerle Deblanc Baker. Jessie was raised with four siblings.

Ben and Jessie were married on November 28, 1911, and had two children: Joseph, who became an attorney in Bay City, Texas, and Lindell, who became a physician and lived in Houston.

The Entzmingers were very active Daytonites. Jessie was a member of the DAR, Eastern Star, the Priscilla Club and the Catholic church. She was also a schoolteacher and instilled her love for education in her children, both of whom graduated from the University of Texas. Jessie would get together with all her friends to make patchwork quilts, which her grandchildren still use today.

Ben worked for Sun Oil Company, in addition to being a rancher, a member of the Methodist Church, a member of Dayton Lodge No. 825, an AF&AM charter member of the Dayton Lions Club and a founding member of Dayton State Bank. He also owned Ben's Meat Market with the phone number of 1. His real love was for his land and his cows. Granddaughter Dorothea Entzminger Baldwin recalls her dad, Lindell, talking about the cattle drives they made to Houston to ship the cows off to Kansas or other locations.

Jessie and Ben Entzminger. *Courtesy of Dorothea Entzminger Baldwin.*

Grandchildren of the Entzmingers remember looking forward to visiting their grandparents. They called their grandfather "Pop" and said he enjoyed playing dominos with his buddies down by the corner store after he retired.

Both grandparents loved to play bridge or canasta. They always had a vegetable garden and would can many of the vegetables for the winter.

Pop made his famous ice box cookies and tapioca whenever they visited. He gave each of them silver dollars on every visit. They were also treated to 10-2-4 Dr. Peppers that were chilled and ready for them to drink. (Their grandparents bought the Dr. Peppers by the wooden case and stored them in their garage).[68]

At Thanksgiving and Christmas, Ben and Jessie made fudge, divinity and huge fruitcakes. Jessie would soak the fruitcakes in cloths containing brandy. Dorothea used to love to listen to them argue about whether the candy was ready or not. She thought it was so much fun riding the sled behind the tractor or riding the tractor with Pop. She said, "We would pick apples off the apple tree or blackberries off the bushes. We usually ate more than we put in the bucket for my grandmother to make pies or jam with, but she would just laugh. And we would go find other bushes to pick from."[69]

Esther Street

Esther Friedman Blonstein (January 31,1906–January 25, 2000), for whom the street is named, was born to Louis and Annie Kaplan Friedman, one of seven children raised in Dayton. Louis arrived in Dayton in 1895 and married Annie in 1901. Louis invested in property all over Dayton, much of which was subdivided and sold as home lots both by himself and his heirs during the 1940s–'60s. Three streets in those subdivisions bear Friedman family names: Esther, Elaine and Susan.

Esther Friedman Blonstein. *Courtesy of the Blonstein Foundation.*

Esther graduated from Dayton High School and CIA College in Denton (Texas Women's University was originally a girl's industrial college and was named College of Industrial Arts & Sciences. It was renamed Texas Women's College in 1934, and in 1957, it received university status).

After college graduation, Esther came back to Dayton and later met and married

Dr. David Blonstein. The Blonsteins moved to Houston, where Esther was an accomplished businesswoman, buying and selling real estate.

She never forgot her Dayton roots. She made donations to purchase some of the first computers at the Jones Public Library and provided many college scholarships for Dayton graduates. Having no children of her own, upon her death, Esther donated her house to Obschestvo Remeslenago Truda (ORT), one of the largest nongovernmental Jewish education and training organizations in the world.[70]

Evelyn Street

Evelyn Street is named for Evelyn Holbrook Waldrop. Her father, A.C. Holbrook Sr., better known as Chester (see Aaron, Chester and Holbrook Streets), owned seventy-four acres of hayfield off Winfree Road that he subdivided and developed in 1962, naming two of the streets after his daughters, Evelyn and Juanita (see Juanita Street).

Evelyn was born in November 1929 in Dayton to A.C. Holbrook Sr. and his wife, Ellen. Her siblings were A.C. Jr., John David, Bruce, Juanita and Virgil "Buddy." She was a 1946 Dayton High School graduate, having served as drum major for the band. She attended one year at Southern Methodist University in 1947.

Evelyn Holbrook Waldrop. *Courtesy of Aaron Holbrook.*

Evelyn married Liberty native Nelson Waldrop on January 8, 1949, and they made their home in Liberty. They bought McLenda Ford Company and reopened it as Waldrop Ford Company in Liberty. While Nelson ran the dealership, Evelyn was a homemaker and raised their two sons, Joe and Allan.[71]

Evelyn enjoyed singing and playing the piano and was an active member of the Valley Players, a local group that continues to perform plays and musicals.[72]

Flowers Street

Jack Flowers. *Courtesy of Adelene Stevens.*

This street was originally named Avenue C.[73] It was renamed for John Edwin "Jack" Flowers. It is one of eleven streets that were renamed by the Dayton City Council in 1961 after Dayton servicemen killed in World War II. Jack was born on October 1, 1919, in Tyler County, Texas, to William Thomas "Tommy" and Mary Barclay Flowers. He was one of seven children and his family moved to Dayton sometime between 1920 and 1927, according to his younger sibling Bill, who was born in Dayton in 1927.[74] Jack attended Dayton schools and left Dayton High School in the tenth grade to enlist in the U.S. Navy.[75]

Jack was an electrician's mate, first class, on the USS *Pickerel* (SS-177) when the submarine was hit and sunk by a depth charge attack off Honshu, Japan, on April 3, 1943. He was twenty-four years old. His name is listed on the Tablets of the Missing at the Honolulu Memorial in Hawaii, and there is a monument to him in Linney Cemetery in Dayton among the Flowerses' graves, although obviously he is not buried there. He received a posthumous Purple Heart.[76]

FM Highway 1960

This highway was originally known as the Eastgate Road because it ran between Dayton and the farming community known as Eastgate, located west of town.

The old road had a different route than it does today. It began at what is today Highway 321, running west for about 6.2 miles, and then curved right onto what is now FM 686. It crossed the railroad tracks and turned left for 1.6 miles to St. Anne's Catholic Cemetery and Church. The road ran straight past the church until it curved left onto what is now CR 623, which intersects present FM 1960 just past the railroad overpass.

Longtime resident Lester Ray Wisegerber remembers the old road well. In 1949, during the Dayton Bronchos football season, he and the team were

This 1918 picture shows the Eastgate Road (now FM Highway 1960). Mr. J.E. Berry's car is stuck in the mud. Two men in the background are bringing a timber to help pry it out. The boy is Berry's grandson, and the other man is unidentified. The automobile is a J.I. Case, the product of the tractor people. *Courtesy of* Texas Illustrated Magazine.

to play a game with Humble High School, and it had rained very hard that day. The school bus headed down Eastgate Road and found that it was too flooded to navigate, so they traveled to Cleveland and wound back around to where the road met the low-water crossing at the San Jacinto River. There was no bridge at the time, and the crossing was too deep for the bus. The football team got out of the bus and walked across the river on the railroad tracks to get to the football field. Lester Ray and his wife, Betty Jo, farmed the rice fields along Eastgate Road in the early 1950s, on both sides of the present railroad overpass.[77]

The Texas Highway Department claimed ownership of the road in approximately 1940, naming it FM 1960, with its western terminus at an intersection with U.S. Highway 290 and State Highway 6 in northwestern Harris County and ending at State Highway 321 in Dayton. The highway was built in sections: to 5.9 miles east of Humble by 1955 and continued to Huffman in 1957. Finally, the route was straightened with the highway ending in Dayton.[78] Locals began referring to the road by its new name, 1960, after the present route was determined.

In the 1970s, FM 1960 was a narrow, two-lane, rutted road that was improved from time to time. In 2012, the highway department constructed a railroad overpass on 1960, 7.2 miles west of Dayton. In 2013, the department greatly improved 1960 by resurfacing and widening it from Highway 321 west to the overpass, adding a center turning lane for a portion of the highway and widening it from one to two lanes on both sides at various locations.

Ford Avenue

Milo and Ella Ford Sr. *Courtesy of Jessica Ford Johnson.*

This street at one time was a county road, but the name changed when it became located in the city limits. It was named for the Ford family, Milo Westel Ford Sr. (1888–1967) and his wife, Ella Fay King (1898–1993), who owned the property around it.

When he was eleven, Milo's family moved to Devers, Texas, from Iowa at the turn of the century to farm rice. As an adult, he moved to the Stilson community outside Dayton and continued to farm for a couple years. His interest was in cattle, so he sold his land in Devers to other rice farmers and pursued his ranching interests. Ella Fay King, whose family moved to the area from North Carolina because her father began rice farming, was teaching school in Kemah at the age of sixteen. She and Milo married in 1917 and both were members of the First United Methodist Church in Dayton.

The Fords bought a newly built wood-frame yellow and red house on present-day South Winfree Street from Ed Pruitt Jr., who had built it for his wife. She did not want to live there, so he sold it furnished with antiques and the surrounding ninety-nine acres for $7,500. Milo bought, raised and sold cattle while Ella raised four children: M.W. Jr., Allene, George David and Minnie Boone, called Boonie and so named because Ella's family were descendants of Daniel Boone. Milo and Ella Ford are buried at Magnolia Park Cemetery in Dayton.[79]

Fordland Estates

This street and the subdivision in which it is found are named for the Ford family (see Ford Avenue and Milo Street). Several years ago, Milo W. Ford Jr., known as M.W., told his daughter, Jessica, and her husband, John Johnson, that he always thought the land behind his house would make a great subdivision but that he was too old to develop it. The Johnsons bought the family land in 2000 after giving great consideration to the subdivision development. John, Jessica and her father decided on the name Fordland Estates. The first phase of building began in 2002 on Ford Road. As of November 2012, phase 3 of the subdivision development will proceed with the addition of forty-nine new housing sites, each covering one-third of an acre.

The Ford family. *Courtesy of Jessica Ford Johnson.*

Jessica Ford Johnson was born December 18, 1959, in Dayton to M.W. Ford Jr. and Dorothy Russell Ford. Her father was born and raised in Dayton, and her mother was from Beaumont. Jessica grew up with an older sister, Gina Fay Ford Bajgier. Jessica was an outgoing student in the Dayton schools and was a cheerleader at Dayton High School, from which she graduated in 1978. She attended Lamar University, graduating in 1988 after having married Sam Mazzu Jr., whom she met at Lamar, and having two children, Sam Anthony Mazzu III and Dorothy Jo Mazzu Landry. The family moved back to Dayton, where their children were raised.

Following her husband's untimely death, Jessica later married John S. Johnson. John was born on January 28, 1952, in Norwich, Connecticut, to Eddie Coke and Minerva Schaeffer Johnson. John's siblings were Pamela Bertha Johnson Ferguson, George Eddie and Samuel Paul Joseph. The Johnsons moved to Richards, Texas, where John graduated from high school in 1970. He received his undergraduate and master's degrees from Sam Houston State University and pursued a career as an educator, both coaching and teaching in Conroe.

Jessica, too, became an educator, teaching math and coaching in Dayton. It was at a basketball tournament in Dayton that Jessica and John met, became friends and eventually married on June 11, 1994. John and his son from a previous marriage, William "BJ" Schaeffer, moved to Dayton where both became active at Dayton High School, BJ as a kicker for the football team and John as assistant principal.

John and Jessica Johnson. *Courtesy of Jessica Ford Johnson.*

Jessica and John continued their education. Jessica received her graduate degree from University of Houston–Clear Lake, and both received doctorate degrees from Nova Southeastern University. Jessica left teaching to become Dayton's curriculum director for several years and continued in administrative positions in the Cleveland and Sheldon school districts. In 2013, Jessica became Dayton Independent School

District school superintendent. John left Dayton High School and held administrative positions at Gulf Coast Alternative School in Liberty and then with the New Caney and Tarkington school districts.

Jessica and John are members of the First United Methodist Church, where John is president of the United Methodist Men's organization and Jessica is church organist (following in her father's footsteps) and children's choir director. Jessica served for several years on the Dayton City Council and is a past president of the Mu Iota Chapter of the Delta Kappa Gamma Society International, a member of the Trinity Valley Exposition Scholarship Committee, Texas Association of School Administrators, the American Cancer Society Relay for Life Committee and Association of Supervision and Curriculum Development.

John is a life member of the Texas High School Coaches' Association. He currently serves on the Dayton City Council and enjoys playing golf, antiquing and hunting. Jessica enjoys traveling, shopping and running. Both are very active members of the Dayton community.[80]

Friery Street

John Friery Jr. *Courtesy of Mary Louise Friery.*

This is another of the eleven streets renamed by the Dayton City Council in 1961 for Dayton servicemen killed in World War II. Originally called Independence Street, it is named after John C. Friery Jr., son of Mr. and Mrs. John C. Friery Sr. He was killed in action on October 21, 1944. He was twenty-seven years old.

Born in 1917, Friery received his junior high education in Madisonville, Texas, and graduated from Dayton High School. Prior to enlisting in service, Friery was an employee of the State Highway Department in Liberty. He enlisted in the U.S. Army in February 1941.

Private First Class Friery trained at Camp Hood, Texas, and Camp Shelby,

Mississippi, and had been overseas with an infantry unit for twenty-five months, seeing action at Guadalcanal, New Guinea, New Georgia, New Caledonia, Toulage and other islands. He was killed in the Pacific and is buried at the Manila American Cemetery at Manila, Philippines.[81] His survivors included his parents, a sister and six brothers.[82]

Glass Street

Glass Street was named for Melinda "Lindy" Glass, a midwife in Dayton who delivered many babies, both black and white. She was born about 1884, according to the 1920 U.S. census, which listed her age as thirty-six.[83] According to Wilbert Wycliff, she was elderly in 1943 when she delivered his and Emily Wycliff's oldest son.[84]

Melinda Glass. *Courtesy of Dayton's Old School Museum.*

Melinda was married twice. The 1920 census lists her husband as Felex Glass, age forty. No children were living with them.[85] Melinda, however, had one child from her first marriage, a daughter named Thema. Thema had two sons, Richard and J.T. Warren, who later lived with their grandmother Melinda.

Melinda attended the Pleasant Hill Baptist Church on Colbert Street and, according to Emily Wycliff, was very personable and sweet and got along with everyone.[86]

Goosecreek Street

Goosecreek Street derived its name from the fact that the old Dayton–Goose Creek Railroad tracks run parallel to it. The community of Goose Creek (now part of Baytown) began to develop in the mid-1830s, around the time of the battle for Texas Independence. In the late 1910s, a rival community was founded on the east side of Goose Creek named Pelly. The community

This engine ran on the Dayton–Goose Creek Railroad, connecting the refineries of Baytown to the Southern Pacific. The engine (#103) operated on the Trinity Valley & Northern, a twenty-mile logging line served by many spurs. Both were railroads founded by former Texas governor Ross Sterling, founder of the Humble Oil and Refining Company. *Courtesy of the* Liberty Vindicator.

of East Baytown was created in the early 1920s. The three consolidated in 1947 to form the town of Baytown.

After an oil strike was made in Tabbs Bay in 1908 at Goose Creek, oil exploration began in earnest. The field became known as the Goose Creek oil field. In 1910, Ross Sterling (see Ross Street), an entrepreneur and visionary, started a venture that developed into the Humble Oil and Refining Company. The drilling continued, and the Goose Creek oil field became the first offshore drilling operation in Texas in 1916. By 1919, the directors of Humble Oil built a refinery in Goose Creek that would become one of the largest and most profitable in the world.[87]

Sterling was also one of the incorporators of the Dayton Lumber Company in 1905, which did much for the development of Dayton, eventually employing 250 people. In 1917, Sterling chartered and built the Dayton–Goose Creek Railroad to move lumber and petroleum products to his Humble Oil and Refining Company. The Dayton–Goose Creek Railroad was the last of the common carriers operating in Liberty County, a very profitable line carrying passengers, oil products and lumber. Sterling sold the rail system to Southern Pacific in 1926.[88]

H–M

Harmon Street

This street, originally called First Avenue,[89] was renamed in 1961, one of eleven streets named for Dayton servicemen killed in World War II. It was named for Geator J. Harmon, born on October 3, 1909, to W.H. and Mattie Harmon. The corporal attended Dayton High School and before enlistment was employed as a mechanic at Neuman Motor Company. According to E.B. Neuman II, son of the owner, Harmon was the body man at the shop, doing all the detailing and body work on the cars and trucks. E.B. was about nine or ten years old when he knew Harmon and said, "He was my idol." E.B. described Harmon as slim and trim, a very friendly, happy guy who took him riding on his motorcycle and made him feel ten feet tall.[90]

Harmon, twenty-six, enlisted in the U.S. Army on May 16, 1942, taking basic training at Sheppard Air Force Base in Wichita Falls, Texas, followed by training in Mission and Fort Worth, Texas, and Guiger Field, Washington. He volunteered for overseas duty and left the States in September 1944.

His parents received word on May 7, 1945, that their son had accidentally drowned while on duty in the Pacific area. The drowning occurred on April 22 when Corporal Harmon was pinned beneath a government vehicle on which he was working. Burial, with full military honors, was at the United

Geator Harmon. *Courtesy of the* Liberty Vindicator.

States Armed Forces Temporary Cemetery in British New Guinea on April 25.[91] Six of his best friends acted as pallbearers. His remains were later flown home, and he was interred at Magnolia Park Cemetery in Dayton.

In a letter accompanying the message from the commanding officer of his headquarters engineering battalion, Geator was highly praised as a splendid soldier of outstanding character, whose loss was deeply felt among his friends and officers. His survivors included his parents; a sister, Mrs. Ethel Matthews; and two brothers, George Harmon and Private Clyde Harmon, who served with the army in France.[92]

Hickory Lane

This street is part of the Linney Creek subdivision. It is not known why the Slovers chose Hickory Lane for the street name.

See Atascocita, Slover Street and Myra Lane sections for more information.

Hill Street

Hill Street is a combination of two previously named streets. The north end was called Depew, and the south end was called Gum.[93] The two were renamed for Knox Charles (K.C.) Hill, who owned the property on which the street is located.[94] K.C.was born on April 13, 1898, in Lavaca County, Texas, to George Johann and Wilhemina Knoble Hill, who were born in Germany. He grew up with eight siblings. The 1900 U.S. census showed the family living in Lavaca County when Knox was two.

By 1910, the Hill family lived in Karnes, Texas, according to census information. Knox was twelve. He received his draft registration card for World War I during 1917–18 while living in Temple, Texas. In 1920, he was twenty-two, living with his mother and four of his siblings in Temple, Bell County,

Texas. While living there, he met and married Alma Mary Lindemann, daughter of Carl Jr. and Malinda Pietzsch Linnemann. Alma was born about 1903 and had two older brothers named Walter and Willie L.

The 1930 census revealed that K.C. and Alma were living in Dayton and had a daughter named Lenora, age two. At this time, K.C.'s occupation was telegraph operator with the steam railroad. His name is written incorrectly in that census as Charles C. Knox.

The family purchased the land between 1930 and 1940, when K.C. and daughter Lenora were listed in the census as living in Houston as boarders. He was married, but Alma was not living with them. K.C. sold his Dayton property in 1944, according to Liberty County Central Appraisal District information.

Until his death in Houston at ninety-two on October 13, 1990, no other information could be found about K.C. Hill. He was buried at Forest Park Cemetery, Houston.[95]

Hillcrest

This street was developed by Mr. Eugene Jansen beginning in 1960 and was so named because it was located at the crest of a hill. Prior to development, the land was the family's home and dairy farm, which Jansen purchased in 1950. The property consisted of one hundred acres and was a beautiful rural place with a huge pecan orchard of forty to fifty trees and several pear trees. Mr. Jansen and his family operated the dairy and also a pig farm. They always had a huge garden, and Mr. Jansen dug a large pond at the far end of the property. In addition to other kinds of animals, he had horses that his children and their friends loved to ride.[96]

Holbrook Street

Holbrook Street is named for Chester and Ellen Holbrook. The street was named in 1962 when Chester developed the Holbrook subdivision on a seventy-four-acre tract of land off North Winfree Street (see Aaron, Chester and Winfree Streets).

Chester liked to say that he was born in Liberty County in 1900 on the prairie west of Dayton under a big Mulberry tree along Wolf Island Road.

Chester and Ellen Holbrook. *Courtesy of Mary Ellen Holbrook Conner.*

His parents, George and Annie Holbrook, lived in a house alongside the Mulberry tree then, but later the family moved to Pasadena, where they grew strawberries on a twenty-acre farm. Chester played football for Milby High School in Harrisburg. In an article in the *Liberty Vindicator* in 1982, he said that he remembered a game against Central High in Houston at Central, which had a new field that hadn't been marked off with lines. Chester got ahold of the ball and took off running for a touchdown, but since there weren't any lines, he couldn't tell when to stop, so he just kept on running. He said he had run half a mile before they finally caught up to him in a Model T and got him to stop.

Chester had a lifelong interest in flying and at age eighty-two, when the *Vindicator* article was written, he was still flying, but he liked to have somebody with him. At that time, his grandson, Allan Waldrop, piloted his plane for him, the third one he had owned.

Among his many other occupations, Chester began farming rice in 1920 with Joe Nelson. They plowed with mules in the beginning, doing all the work by hand. Chester married Ellen Elizabeth Nelson in 1922, the daughter of a pioneer Liberty County rice farmer. Ellen moved to Dayton from Iowa with her parents, Carl David and Anna Nelson, when she was two years old. She attended Dayton's schools, graduating in 1918.

In the *Vindicator* article, she was asked if she helped with the farming after her marriage, and she said, "My job was to cook for the hands, and that was a job! I cooked the dinners, and we took them out to the field in a wagon pulled by mules. I had help with it. I didn't go to the field with the dinner all the time, but sometimes I did go."[97]

Granddaughter Mary Ellen Holbrook Conner said that the entire family gathered every Sunday and holidays at her grandparents' home for dinner. The family was a large one, including Chester and Ellen's six children, A.C. Jr., Bruce, Evelyn Holbrook Waldrop, Juanita Holbrook Rizzo, Buddy and John David; their spouses; and all their children. Mary Ellen said that every Saturday, her grandmother would also go visit her sister Ruth and go to the grocery store. She was a member of the First United Methodist Church.[98]

Ellen Holbrook died on January 31, 1987,[99] and Chester followed on February 21, 1990.[100] They are buried at Magnolia Park Cemetery in Dayton.

Holitzke Street

This street is one of eleven that were renamed in 1961 by the Dayton City Council in honor of Dayton soldiers killed in World War II. Holitzke Street is named for Joseph L. Holitzke, born in 1915, son of Mr. and Mrs. Mike Holitzke of the Eastgate community. Joseph grew up with three brothers and five sisters and was a 1934 graduate of Dayton High School. He was employed by Hydril Company in Houston before entering service with the U.S. Air Corps in September 1942.

Joseph Holitzke. *Courtesy of the* Liberty Vindicator.

Sergeant Holitzke, first engineer and gunner on a Liberator bomber named "Phony Express," participated in the invasion of France on June 6 with the Eighth Air Force operating from England. He had been abroad since April 26 and had recently received the Air Medal for his achievements with the Eighth Air Force. The citation was issued from England by Brigadier General Hodges, calling attention to Sergeant Holitzke's "meritorious achievements in accomplishing with distinction several aerial operational missions over enemy-occupied continental Europe. The courage, coolness, and skill displayed by him in the face of determined opposition materially aided in the successful completion of these missions. His actions reflect great credit upon himself and the armed forces of the United States."

Joseph, age twenty-nine, was killed in action over England on July 13, according to a War Department message received by his wife, the former Martha Ann Navatil of Dayton. In addition to his parents and wife, Joseph left behind an infant son named Don Joseph, three brothers and five sisters.[101]

In February 1945, Martha Holitzke and her son Don Joseph traveled to Ellington Field in Houston, where they were presented another Air Medal and two Oak Leaf Clusters in honor of her husband. Other awards made to Holitzke were a Presidential Unit Citation, a Purple Heart and a citation from Governor Coke Stevenson.[102] Holitzke is buried in the Cambridge American Cemetery at Cambridge, England.[103] A memorial service was held in Dayton at the First United Methodist Church.

Holmes Street

This street is named for Johnnie Lee Holmes, who had a home located on this road for many years.[104] He was born on August 13, 1902, to Louis M. (1878–1958) and Emily Ann (1875–1943) Holmes. In the 1910 U.S. census, the Holmes family was living in Chambers County, and four children were listed, the oldest of whom was Johnnie, age seven.

By 1920, the family was living in Liberty and included six children. Johnnie was seventeen years old. As of the 1930 census, he had married a lady named Irene and his occupation was carpenter. They were living in Dayton with no children.

The 1940 census revealed that Johnnie went to school through the sixth grade, and Maylon Fabriquze, age eighteen and presumably Irene's son, was living with him and Irene. Johnnie's listed occupation was construction contractor. Another document showed that Johnnie Holmes enlisted in the U.S. Army as a private on September 26, 1942, for the duration of World War II.

Johnnie Holmes passed away on October 18, 1972, at the age of seventy and is buried at Ryan Cemetery in Tarkington Prairie in the family plot alongside his mother and father. On his death document, Johnnie was listed as widower. No information was found about the death of Irene or where she is buried.[105]

Houston Street

Houston Street, originally named Akron,[106] was one of the main thoroughfares in Dayton before 1910 because of the large two-story school built there in 1909 and because it was the road one took to connect with other roads to go to Houston (the OST, now U.S. Highway 90, didn't come through Dayton until after 1922). The street runs east–west in the general direction of Houston and honors the memory of General Sam Houston, who maintained a summer home near present-day Beach City in Chambers County.[107]

No one remembers when the street was named, just that it was always called Houston Street. Lester Ray Wisegerber lived in his great-grandparents' house on West Houston as a boy in the late 1930s (behind where RaceWay gas station is today). He said the road had a shell surface then and flooded badly when it rained. In the early 1950s, the street had a gravel surface.

One of Lester Ray's memories of living there was that it was his job as a young child of about six years old to take the family cow, Mary Frances, to the end of the street (toward present-day Highway 146) and stake it so it could graze. Then in the evening, he would take the cow home so his mother could milk it.[108] Much later, Lester Ray and his wife, Betty Jo George, and children lived in the same house, and the children would watch Dayton Bronco football games by standing on a fence across the street, the football stadium having been built on Houston Street.[109]

Houston Street continues to be important to the community as it is the southern boundary of the U.S. Post Office building, the location of the Old School Museum and the first location of the Jones Public Library (now the Dayton ISD Educational Support Center).

Hunnicutt Street

Hunnicutt Street is named for James D. and Anna Gray Slade Hunnicutt, who moved to Dayton between 1880 and 1900. James Hunnicutt was born in March 1853 in Mississippi to Madison and Ezula Hunnicutt. In 1860 at age seven, James was living with his parents and six siblings in Kemper, Mississippi. Anna Gray Slade was born in September 1858 in Alabama to Thomas Blount and Catherine Irby Comegys Slade. James and Anna married in 1880, and the U.S. census that year showed they lived in Springfield, Alabama, where James was a telegraph operator.

By the census of 1900, the Hunnicutts were living in Dayton and had nine children: Cottie, born in 1882; James D. Jr., born in 1884; Maddell, born in 1887; Annie Gray, born in 1889; Edwina, born in 1892; Perry, born in 1895; Julian D. and Bulla, born in 1896; and Grace D., born in 1901.[110]

According to longtime local resident Joann Paul, Hunnicutt was instrumental in developing the French Settlement area north of town where an influx of French "Cajuns" settled and where Hunnicutt Street is located.[111] In the 1910 census, the couple had four of their children living at home: James D. Jr., Annie G., Perry and Grace D. Lifelong resident Bobby Harris said that Mr. Hunnicutt sold lots from land he owned sometime in the 1910s.

Prior to 1920, the Hunnicutts bought and operated the Hunnicutt Hotel, which was located across the street from the train depot.[112] The census that year lists twelve boarders of the hotel in addition to the family members. In *The Sheaf* yearbook of 1920, Mrs. J.D. Hunnicutt is listed as a member of the parent-teacher association.

Anna died in Dayton in 1930 at the age of seventy-two. James Hunnicutt died in 1940 in Dayton at the age of eighty-seven. Both are buried at Linney Cemetery in Dayton.

Jamison Street

Jamison Street was named for William Thomas and Allene Jamison and is one of the streets in the Suburban Acres subdivision. They owned the land from which the subdivision was created in 1964.

W.T. was born on September 22, 1878, in Brazoria County, Texas, near Oyster Creek outside Angleton and died in Dayton on April 15, 1962. He married Allene Solomon on April 18, 1917, in Dayton. Allene was born on July 30, 1889, at Alto, Texas, and died in Dayton on December 28, 1973.

W.T. was the son of William Jamison and Sarah Sloan, Irish immigrants from County Tyrone. William's twin brother, Samuel, and brother James

W.T. Jamison. *Courtesy of Dayton's Old School Museum.*

were the first in his family to come to America. Samuel settled somewhere in Kansas, and James came to Texas and settled in Brazoria County about 1840. Later, brothers Thomas and William came to join James in Texas. They enjoyed the American dream, working hard, at first for others, before acquiring land and becoming prosperous cattle ranchers in Brazoria County.

Allene was the daughter of Emmett Wales Solomon and his wife, Mamie Allen. Emmett was a Methodist minister who served many congregations in Texas and, in his early years, was a circuit rider, traveling from one small town to another, holding services and spreading Methodism. He was a dynamic speaker and is still well remembered in the history of the Methodist church in Texas.

W.T. received an associate degree in business from Angleton Business College, and Allene received a teaching degree from Sam Houston Normal Institute, as it was known at that time. As a young man, W.T. and his cousin Morris Jamison moved to Humble, Texas, where they formed a partnership and opened a feed store. It was during this time that W.T. became good friends with area businessman and future governor Ross Sterling. W.T. was quite successful running his feed store enterprise, and Sterling, having newly acquired several small banks in southeast Texas, including one in Dayton, asked W.T. if he would like to move to Dayton and manage that bank branch. W.T. Jamison moved to Dayton around 1907, initially sleeping in the bank. It was a one-man operation, with W.T. doing everything from janitorial work to bookkeeping and teller duties. Eventually, he became president of the bank and served in that capacity until his death. He founded Jamison Insurance Agency in 1908. During his career as a banker, W.T., who still loved ranching,

Allene Jamison. *Courtesy of Mary Beth Jamison.*

kept a large herd of cattle and enjoyed being a cowboy in the afternoons and weekends.

Allene Solomon moved to Dayton to accept a teaching position at Dayton High School. She was an accomplished musician and hostess, a member of the Egg Circle, Priscilla Club and Stitch and Chatter Club. During World War II, she was a volunteer aircraft "spotter," manning a tower five miles south of Dayton on FM 1409.

W.T. and Allene married in 1917 and raised five children: Louise Jamison Clark, Allene Jamison Hodges, Dorothy Jamison Tate, W.T. "Bill" Jr. and James Robert "Bob."

W.T. died April 15, 1962. After the death of their father and to help their mother, Allene, with an estate tax liability, the children formed a partnership called Suburban Acres and subdivided acreage located on North Winfree Street, which they sold as residential home sites.

Allene died on December 28, 1973. Along with her husband, she is buried at Magnolia Park Cemetery in Dayton.[113]

Juanita Street

This street is named for Juanita Holbrook Rizzo. Juanita's father, A.C. Holbrook Sr., better known as Chester (see Aaron, Chester and Holbrook Streets), met with the Dayton City Council on June 12, 1961, to discuss subdividing forty-one acres that he owned off Winfree Road. The development of this hay field, known as the Holbrook subdivision, began in 1962.

Juanita Holbrook Rizzo. *Courtesy of Aaron Holbrook.*

Juanita was born in February 1935 in Dayton to Ellen and Chester Holbrook. Her siblings were A.C. Jr., John David, Evelyn, Bruce and Virgil "Buddy." She was a Dayton High School cheerleader, graduating in 1952. Juanita was an accomplished pianist and graduated from Southern Methodist University in 1956 with a major in music.

Juanita married Liberty native Sam Rizzo on October 26, 1947, and had four children: Sam Jr., Dan, David and Elizabeth Rizzo Moore. In 1960, Juanita and her family moved to Houston, where Sam pursued a career as a CPA. Juanita played the organ for a Catholic church in Houston for many years. As of this writing, Juanita and Sam are retired and raise Angus cattle in Madisonville, Texas.[114]

Kay Street

Kay Street was originally called Cato,[115] though it was later known by two names. The street is divided by Winfree Street, with the west side called Texas Avenue and the east side called Avenue B.[116] It is one of eleven streets renamed by the Dayton City Council in 1961 for Dayton servicemen killed in World War II. The street is named for Clyde David Kay, son of William Seth and Clara Kay. He had one sister, Odell, and two half sisters, Crystal Jackson and Anita Symmank.

The Dayton High School yearbook for 1937–38 listed Clyde as a fullback with the Dayton Broncos, writing, "He was well liked by all the boys and girls and they will be sorry to lose him next year." Clyde is described by Edith Grantham, who knew him when she was a child, as a "fun type of guy who liked being with friends."[117] He loved watching and participating in bull riding. When his family moved to Anahuac in his junior year of high school, Clyde chose to stay in Dayton so that he could finish high school there and lived in the home of Mr. and Mrs. Leo Moreau.[118] Serving as

Clyde Kay. *Courtesy of the* Liberty Vindicator.

a surrogate mom to Clyde, Mrs. Moreau was devastated by his death. She honored his memory by writing a poem about him.

Clyde had enlisted in the U.S. Marine Corp in January 1942 and trained in San Diego, California. He was sent overseas in January 1943 and saw action in some of the fiercest battles in the South Pacific. It is known that he participated in the Battle of Tarawa without injury. Clyde was killed in action while serving with the second division of the marine corps on the island of Saipan, according to a notice released on July 11, 1944, by the War Department.

Clyde David Kay is listed on the Honolulu Memorial at Honolulu, Hawaii. He posthumously received a Bronze Star and a Purple Heart.[119]

Written in memory of Clyde D. Kay
by Just another "Mom"—Mrs. Leo Moreau

Years ago he came to our house to live,
We learned to care for him with all the love we had to give.
Today he sleeps beneath the war torn Pacific skies
God called him home while in his countries service once more to rise.
He was a bold sort of lad,
No years of life or death he had.
We will miss him oh so very much,
Especially his Mom, who learned to feel his gentle touch.
Life's work on earth for him is complete for today
Oh! God when I kneel down, help me for him to pray.[120]

Kerr Street

Kerr Street is named for Andrew Erastus Kerr, referred to in publications as A.E. Kerr. A.E. was born on January 31, 1876, in Johnson County, Texas, to his father, B.B., and mother, D.E. Kerr, according to the 1880 U.S. census records. He had a younger brother, W.E. Kerr. Between 1881 and 1888, his mother married a man named J.T. Wilson. Their marriage produced a son born in 1889 named W.A. Wilson. A.E. was still living with his mother and stepfather at the time of the 1900 census at age twenty-five.

On November 25, 1902, A.E. married Leonora Pitts in Grandview, Johnson County, Texas. Leonora, daughter of Robert and Martha Pegueus Pitts, was born on January 25, 1880 in Pontotoc, Mississippi. The Kerrs had three children: A.E. Kerr Jr., Robert and Oma.[121]

It is believed that the Kerr family moved to Dayton between 1910 and 1912, although they don't show up on the 1910 census record. A.E. Kerr had a long association with Ross Sterling (see Ross Street), who was instrumental in Dayton's early development. When the Dayton Lumber Company fell on hard times in 1912 and went into receivership, Sterling and others reorganized the company with Sterling as the new president and Kerr as secretary and resident manager. The new owners changed the name to Dayton Mills Company.[122]

Sterling also tapped Kerr as his vice-president and general manager of the Dayton–Goose Creek Railroad that he founded in 1917. When Sterling closed the Dayton mill in 1920, he moved the Kerrs to Houston to help manage his other widespread interests. Kerr subsequently became president of the Houston National Bank and president of the Citizens State Bank of Baytown, which he helped organize.

A.E. Kerr died on January 4, 1967,[123] preceded by Leonora on May 27, 1966.

Kindt Street

Kindt Street was named for Abraham F. Kindt, known as Abe, born on March 4, 1847, in Ohio. His father's name was also Abraham (1801–1884), but his mother is not known to the author. It also isn't known if Abe ever lived in Dayton, but he was known locally as a pioneer land broker.[124]

In the 1870 U.S. Census, Abe, age twenty-three, was living in Wolf River, Kansas, with his older brother Josiah and his father. His occupation was listed as farmer.[125] The 1880 census showed him living in Belleville, Kansas, still farming at age thirty-three and single.

A search of the deeds at the Liberty County Courthouse revealed that the Corporation of Liberty City sold to Abraham F. Kindt forty-eight acres in block 38 of Dayton on July 11, 1893. That area became known and is still known today as the Kindt subdivision.[126]

Upon the death of Abe on December 15, 1915, his estate, which included $20,000–$25,000 worth of property, was left to his church in Lawton, Oklahoma, the First Church of Christ Scientist. The newspaper in the town reported:

> *After a day's deliberation, the jury in the Josah* [sic] *Kindt case which has occupied the attention of the district court this week, returned a verdict for Josiah and Henry Kindt, brothers of the deceased, thus breaking the will of Abe Kindt who left $20,000 worth of property to the Christian Science Church of this city. The jury in their findings reported that Kindt was capable of making a will, but that they believed that he had been unduly influenced. The case has attracted much attention. When the church will appeal the case has not been stated at this time.*[127]

In 1921, the newspaper reported that Abe's will was upheld by the Supreme Court and the church would indeed inherit his estate.[128]

On February 14, 1925, J.D. Hunnicutt (see Hunnicutt Street) filed a deed at the Liberty County Courthouse showing that he bought the Kindt property from the First Church of Christ Scientist.[129] He sold the same property to John Gaillard, who began subdividing it into lots for homes in 1930. Gaillard filed the plat of the Kindt subdivision at the courthouse on April 3, 1930.[130]

Abraham F. Kindt is buried at Highland Cemetery in Lawton, Comanche County, Oklahoma.

Klemp Road

This road was constructed about 1969 and named after the Klemp Corporation, a manufacturing company, who leased the plant built at the end of the road. The Dayton Industrial Foundation, formed in 1969, built the half-million-dollar plant on a seven-acre portion of a new industrial park that was developed a mile west of town off FM 1960.[131]

The foundation negotiated with Klemp, a manufacturer of custom grating primarily marketed in Texas and the Southwest, to begin production in Dayton. The president of the Klemp Corporation was Lee Shelly, and its attorney was Earl Deutsch.

The Dayton Industrial Foundation's executive director and attorney was Robert S. Tucker (see Tucker Street). Other members of the foundation were J.E. Berry, president; W.A. Conner, board chairman; Johnny E. Lindsey, vice-president; and James Leard Conner, secretary-treasurer.[132]

The Klemp Corporation sold to American Metals in later years, but the name of the road remained.

LaBlanc Lane

This road is named for June and Mary LeBlanc, who made their home there for many years. The street sign is a misspelling of their name, which often happens through human error. Manual June LeBlanc was born in Abbeville, Louisiana, to Arthur and Edolie LeBlanc on November 18, 1900, and grew up with four brothers and two sisters. June's career was spent working on pipelines for various companies, which required traveling the country.

Mary Frances Lauderdale was born on March 10, 1922, close to Groesbeck, Texas, to Horace and Zelda Croft Lauderdale, and she grew up with two brothers. She attended a country school through her elementary years and then went to high school in Groesbeck. Mary worked as a telephone operator in her home town after her school years, and it was in Groesbeck that she met June. He was working on a pipeline through town, and one of his co-workers, who was also a friend of Mary's, introduced them. They were married in 1940.

Following their marriage, Mary became a homemaker and traveled with June for his job, living in Ohio, Maryland, New Hampshire and other places. They made their home in Baytown, Texas, for several years before moving to Dayton in 1952. June had previously bought 140 acres of land with a house, and it was there that they settled down permanently.

The road now called LaBlanc was originally accessed from North Winfree Street, with no access to State Highway 321. Sometime in the 1960s, the bridge on the road washed out, so the county cut a route to continue the road to intersect State Highway 321. As of that time, cars could no longer access the road from Winfree.

In 1968, Johnny and Sue Moore bought land from the LeBlancs on which to build their house. Another couple, the Otts, were living on some of the property prior to their arrival. About 1973, Mary was trying to come up

Mary and June LeBlanc. *Courtesy of Mary LeBlanc.*

with a name for the road and asked Sue to help her. Sue said she thought LeBlanc Lane sounded good, so Mary turned in the name to the city, which erected a street sign. Years later, when many roads received county road designations, the LeBlanc Lane sign was removed. Mary called the city and insisted that it be put back into place. So a new sign was ordered, and the street name came back misspelled, hence LaBlanc.

Mary described June as a quiet, stay-at-home man who enjoyed watching television. June was Catholic and had three children by a previous marriage. He passed away on November 28, 1978, and is buried at Magnolia Park Cemetery in Dayton.

As of this writing, Mary is living at Magnolia Place Care Center in Liberty, but she still maintains her home on LaBlanc Lane. She is a member of Grace Community Baptist Church in Dayton and volunteered her time to fold the church bulletins each week for Sunday worship. In her more active years, Mary enjoyed quilting.[133] Sue Moore said the LeBlancs were good neighbors.[134]

LaCour Street

Carey LaCour. *Courtesy of Dayton's Old School Museum.*

LaCour Street is named after Carey Carl LaCour, son of Will LaCour (1882–1968) and Mamie P. LaCour-Smith (1887–1975). He was born on July 18, 1905, in Dayton and grew up with one sister, Maydee Smith Prater, and a brother, Percy LaCour. Carey married Everlean Smith in 1950, who had two children prior to the marriage: Thesolona Smith and Annie Wingo. The couple had a son, Carey Lacour Jr.[135]

LaCour worked for the constable's office with the City of Dayton during the 1950s and was appointed by Dayton City Council as humane officer in 1959. He also worked as a janitor at the Colbert School, retiring in the 1960s. He was described by friends Hurley Provost and Henry Dugat as being friendly, very comical and somewhat moody.[136]

Carey's home was located on the street bearing his name. He passed away in January 1983 at the age of seventy-seven. He is buried at Acie Cemetery in Dayton.

Ladd Street

Ladd Street is named for E.P. Ladd Sr. of Arkansas, who was a major stockholder in the Dayton Lumber Company when it was organized in December 1905. The company did more to develop the town than anything else at the time. Ladd never resided in Dayton, but he kept a monetary interest in the lumber company until 1920, when he and the other owners sold it (the name was changed to Dayton Mills Company in 1915) to the South Texas Hardwood Company of Harris County.[137] Other prominent men with the company, such as A.E. Kerr, R.B. Edgar and Ross Sterling, have Dayton streets named after them also.

Elmer Pierpoint Ladd was born on April 22, 1863, in Illinois to John and Mary Lynch Ladd. According to the 1870 U.S. census, at age seven, he was living in Little Rock, Arkansas, with his parents and brother Jesse, age three. In 1889, he married Josephine "Josie" Phillips (b. 1870) in Conway, Arkansas. The couple had a son, Walter Ernest Ladd, born in 1895.

The 1897–98 Little Rock, Arkansas City Directory listed E.P. Ladd as a resident and his occupation as "shingles." By 1900, the Ladds were living in Melton, Arkansas, and E.P. was in the lumber manufacturing business. How he came to be an investor with the Dayton Lumber Company in 1905 isn't known, but another investor from Arkansas, J.J. Kress, was listed along with him.

He was a member of the Pine Bluff (Arkansas) Auto Club of 1905, which consisted of seven automobiles. According to an online article, the automobiles created quite a stir. Citizens were advised that the best way to see the cars would be on Fifth or Sixth Avenue from four to six o'clock in the evenings. The seven cars were to drive to Little Rock and return. The trip would take three days: one day up, one day to rest and one day home. Members of the Auto Club were Dr. A.G. Thompson, O.M. Kilroy, L.O. Knox, F.G. Smart, W.R. Crawford, E.P. Ladd, E.C. Stowell and Dr. B.D. Luck.[138]

Another newspaper article in the Gentry, Arkansas *Journal-Advance*, on November 15, 1907, reported: "E.P. Ladd, president of the Little Rock Automobile Company, has been arrested and placed in jail at Pine Bluff, on a bench warrant charging him with the murder of John Scott, a sawyer, at Ladd,

Pine Bluff Auto Club, 1905. E.P. Ladd is in the center auto. *Courtesy of the* Journal-Advance.

Ark., November, 1905. He was indicted by the Jefferson County grand jury, it being the fifth that had convened since the death of Scott. Some time ago Mrs. Scott sued Ladd for $50,000 in the federal court and obtained a judgment for $10,000 which amount Ladd paid. He claims self-defense as a motive."

The *Montgomery (MI) Tribune* reported on May 21, 1909:

> *With remarkable rapidity the jury in the case of the state against E.P. Ladd of Little Rock, former treasurer of the Arkansas Good Roads Association, acquitted the defendant in the Jefferson circuit court. Ladd shot and killed John Scott, a sawyer in his employ, at Ladd, Ark., October 24, 1905. Mrs. Scott, widow of the man Ladd killed, obtained a judgment for $10,000 in the federal court against Ladd for the death of her husband. The judgment was paid. Mrs. Scott now lives in Arrabi, Colorado, but came here and testified against Ladd.*

Sometime prior to 1918, E.P. and Josie divorced, and he then married Myrtle Lou (1878–1950). They had a son, Elmer Pierpoint Ladd Jr., who was born in 1919. The 1920 census showed the family living in Cane Creek, Arkansas and E.P. listed his occupation as merchant and planter. By the 1930 census, E.P., age sixty, listed his occupation as farmer. He and his family continued to live in Cane Creek.

E.P. Ladd died on August 28, 1942, and is buried in Little Rock, Arkansas.[139]

Laird Street

Laird Street is named for Morgan J. Laird, born on May 15, 1908, in Stacy, Texas, to Henry and Ida Lee Laird. He grew up among siblings James, Harry, Raymon, Robert, Alice and Helen. Laird's career began with the Cranfill-Reynolds Drilling Company in 1929, the same year he married Mary Dee Riley on June 23. He was transferred to the Esperson Dome Oil Field, west of Dayton, in 1930. The company was reorganized in 1933, with the name becoming General Crude Oil Company.

Mary Laird, a homemaker, raised their children, Jackie, Morgan Jr., Sidney and Curtis. The family moved to Dayton in 1959. Morgan established a long-lasting working relationship between the oil company and the farmers and cattlemen in and around the Esperson Dome Oil Field. One of his close friends was Chester Holbrook (see Aaron, Chester and Holbrook Streets), who in 1962 began developing a new subdivision involving a seventy-four-acre tract of land. He named most of the streets after family members, but he named Laird Street in honor of his friend.

Morgan Laird. *Courtesy of Curtis Laird.*

Morgan retired from General Crude in 1973, pursuing his interests in hunting and fishing. His greatest passion, though, was being with his grandchildren. He passed away on November 9, 1981, preceded by his wife, Mary, on April 17, 1979. They are buried in Magnolia Park Cemetery in Dayton.[140]

Lawrence Street

Lawrence Street, originally named Cypress Street in 1957 when the Dayton Heights subdivision was created by the Trinity Development Company, was renamed at some point after James Visage "J.V." Sr. and Winnefred Rachael Key Lawrence, who came to Dayton in either 1919 or 1920.

Winnefred and J.V. Lawrence. *Courtesy of Teresa Lawrence.*

J.V. Lawrence Sr. was born on December 28, 1878, in Thomaston, Dewitt County, Texas, to Jacob Lewis and Nancy Green Lawrence. He was listed as the only child of his parents in the 1880 U.S. census, and his father's occupation was recorded as farmer. Soon thereafter, siblings were born to the family: Calvin Benton (1881), Romeo Lafayette (1883), Joseph William (?) and Mollie Elizabeth (1887). In the 1900 census, J.V., age twenty-one, was single and still living in Thomaston, working as a farm laborer.

J.V. married Winnefred Rachael Key on July 19, 1904, in Normanna, Bee County, Texas. Winnefred was born on April 4, 1882, in Bedias, Grimes County, Texas, to Christopher Eureka and Sallie Sanders Key. Prior to their marriage, Winnefred taught guitar classes. J.V. and Winnefred had their first child in 1906, naming him Joseph Benton Lawrence. A daughter, Eunice Opal, was born in 1907.

The 1910 census showed the family living in Normanna, with J.V.'s occupation listed as blacksmith. J.V. was thirty-one, Winnefred was twenty-six, Joseph was four and Eunice was two years old. The family continued to grow with Helena "Lena" born in 1910, James V. Lawrence Jr. born in 1912 and Herbert "Alvin" born in 1916. J.V. Lawrence Sr. received his draft registration card for World War I in the year 1917–18 at San Patricio County, Texas.

By 1920, the family was living in Dayton, and J.V.'s occupation was carpenter. The census listed five children. Another son, Gerald "Jerry" K., was born in 1923, and Sallie June was born in 1926.

The decade of the 1930s was very busy for J.V. The 1930 census gave his occupation as manager of City Water Works for the City of Dayton.[141] The city council minutes of January 2, 1930, showed that W.B. Jamison and J.V. Lawrence (assessor and collector) were appointed to a purchasing committee of the council. The minutes of April 3, 1930, listed J.V. Lawrence, fire marshal, in attendance, even though he was officially appointed as such on August 7 of that year. The minutes of April 14, 1930, showed that J.V. Lawrence was to be in charge of all city work including waterworks, streets and bridges. Lastly, he was mentioned as in attendance of the February 5, 1939 city council meeting as waterworks superintendent.

In addition to his work with the city, J.V. also operated a blacksmith shop that opened in 1936. He ran a sheet metal shop and hardware store located on the southwest corner of Cook and Church Streets. A picture published in one of the local newspapers was found at the Old School Museum in Dayton. It shows the interior of Lawrence's blacksmith shop with J.V. in the foreground and Felix Bernard in the background.

In the last census available, 1940, the Lawrence family had only one child living at home: Jerry, age seventeen. J.V. was sixty-one, and Winnefred was fifty-eight. J.V.'s occupation was listed as proprietor of a hardware store. J.V. passed away on May 26, 1962, in Dayton. Winnefred passed away on November 10, 1979, in Freeport, Brazoria County, Texas. Both are buried at Forest Park Cemetery in Houston.[142]

Teresa Lawrence's family (the Alvin Lawrences) lived next door to her grandparents on South Church Street. The grandchildren called J.V. "PawPaw," and Winnefred they called "MawMaw." Teresa remembers them both as very sweet, giving people. PawPaw and MawMaw were members of the First Baptist Church. They loved music and were always playing the radio. They had family get-togethers in the yard under the pecan trees with long white wooden tables filled with food. Teresa remembers celebrating birthdays on those same tables under the trees.

Herb Lawrence, Teresa's brother, has a particular memory of needing five dollars so that he could go to town to the Dime Store. He believed he could purchase anything in the store if he had five dollars. No one would "loan" him the money, so he went to PawPaw and told him he needed five dollars. PawPaw gave him the money and then asked what he wanted to buy. Herb didn't know exactly but told him that he thought he could buy anything in the store. PawPaw took back the money.[143]

Ligons Street

Harry Ligons Sr. *Courtesy of Burley Ligons Gant.*

Ligons Street is named for Harry Dennis Ligons Sr., who was born in Nigton, Texas, on August 12, 1884, to Christopher and Eliza Williams Ligons. His obituary said, "He traveled near and far, then moved to Dayton, Texas where he met and married Mary Lee Love on July 1, 1916."

Mary Lee was born in Brenham, Texas. Their marriage produced ten children: five boys (Mayfield, Henry L., Earcell, Harry Jr. and O.T.) and five girls (Jessie Mae, Leslie Lee, Eliza, Mary Lee and Geneva).

Dennis was a carpenter, and he was a very learned gentleman, according to Dayton resident Joann Paul. The Ligons were faithful and active members of the Mt. Pleasant Baptist Church, where Dennis was a deacon.[144] He was also active in the community. According to his family, Dennis Ligons was a quiet person, but when he talked, he always had positive things to say. He gave very good advice and read the Bible.

The Ligons family lived on the street that bears their name, and a family cemetery was established on the property. Dennis Ligons was buried there after he passed away on October 25, 1981. At his death, he left behind nine children (he was preceded in death by a daughter), thirty-six grandchildren, fifty-two great-grandchildren and fourteen great-great-grandchildren.[145]

Linney Street

Linney Street is named after the Michael Linney family, early residents of West Liberty, as Dayton was known until the mid-1880s.

Michael Linney was born on October 24, 1800, in Wayne County, Kentucky. He immigrated to the Ayish Bayou District of Texas in 1823 with his father, Henry (Hugh) Linney, accompanied by his brother Charles and sister Rebecca, and registered with the Mexican government. He lived there for at least eleven years. Henry Linney was a widower at that time.

Sometime after his arrival to Texas, Michael Linney married Elizabeth Weeks, who was born in 1808 in Louisiana. They lived for a while in East Texas, and their first child, John (1828–1902), was born near the Angelina River. When the Texas Revolution became eminent, the family moved to Catahoula Parish in Louisiana, where Henry Hugh Linney died in 1834, leaving his estate to his two sons, Michael and Charles.

Michael and Elizabeth's other children were born in Catahoula Parish: Rebecca Linney Pruett (1830–1885) [see Pruitt Street], Mary Linney Peloquin (1832–1905), Elizabeth Linney Gill (1836–1870), Henry Edmund Linney (1837–1918), Nancy Linney Peloquin (1841–?) and Martha Linney Toups (1842–1908).

Ferry crossing Trinity River carrying unidentified people. *Courtesy of* Texas Illustrated Magazine.

Michael Linney moved his family to Liberty County, Texas, in 1842, acquiring land on the west side of the Trinity River and residing in West Liberty. He was, for a time, engaged in operating the ferry across the Trinity River. According to the minutes of the board of trustees for Liberty, "On April 21, 1860, the Liberty ferry was leased by the Board of Trustees of the town of Liberty to Michael Linney for four years for three hundred and twenty dollars."[146] Michael was a farmer and a stock raiser by occupation, continuing to accumulate land and running cattle and hogs throughout the river bottom. Early residents named Linney Creek after the family.

Elizabeth Weeks Linney died on September 10, 1862, and Michael Linney died on November 22, 1871. For reasons unknown, both are buried at the French Cemetery in Dayton. The Linney Cemetery is located in Dayton, and it is not known if the cemetery began as a family cemetery or was simply named for the family. It is claimed that the cemetery began in the 1850s, but the gravestones date from the 1880s, with earlier burials unmarked. One of the earliest marked gravestones is for Joseph Monroe Linney, who died at the age of six days in 1880. Other early marked gravestones include Jane Francis Hunt in 1881 and Marie Louise Schneider Gossie in 1885.[147] Many descendants of the Linneys have continued to live in Dayton, most of whom are buried at Linney Cemetery.

Lisa Lane

Lisa Wilson. *Courtesy of Lisa Wilson.*

Troi Lisa Wilson, known as Lisa, was born on July 16, 1960, in Dayton to Troy and Nina Wilson. She grew up with sisters Susan and Laura and brother Tony. This street was named for Lisa because her father, who developed it, knew that a Susan Street already existed, and he thought there was also a Laura Street. The sisters remember that as children, they had the job of pulling up roots and picking up sticks to help clear the land.

Troy Wilson bought the property from the Dayton Future Farmers of America organization and developed several streets. Right before their wedding, Troy and Nina were clearing land, with Troy on a tractor and Nina resting on a gate. Troy turned the tractor very quickly, hitting the gate and breaking Nina's leg. They had to postpone the wedding until she could recover.

Lisa, graduated from Dayton High School in 1978 and from Stephen F. Austin State University in 1990. She married Andy Gibson in 1984, and they had two children, Abby and Matt. Lisa taught piano lessons and enjoys playing the piano. She completed twenty-one years of teaching in public schools as of this writing, first teaching in Dibol, then in Nacogdoches and in Port Boliver. She currently teaches math at Liberty Middle School in Liberty, Texas. Lisa's favorite thing is enjoying the company of her grandson, Grey Gibson Taylor.[148]

Little John

This street in the Sherwood subdivision was developed by Bobby and Joe Harris beginning in 1955. When considering what to name the streets in the subdivision, they found an area of Houston that had nice homes and had streets named Little John and Sherwood. They liked the sound of those names and since they were building custom homes, those were the street names they chose. Little John was the fourth phase of the subdivision project, the first three being extensions of Sherwood Drive.[149]

Lovers Lane

Lovers Lane was so named because it was a popular destination for young couples desiring a bit of privacy. Its secluded location south of town on a dark, dead-end dirt road helped ensure that privacy—that is, until the residents of Dayton passed a bond election in 2008 under the mayorship of Steve Stephens to build a new city library/community center with concrete streets, sidewalks, curbs and gutters. In addition to paving the south end of Cleveland Street where the library/community center was to be located, the paving project also included West Luke Street (an extension of Luke Street on the east side of Highway 1409) and Lovers Lane.

A company named Stone Creek Homes, owned and operated by Peter Merritt and Chris Henrich, purchased twenty acres on West Luke Street and

Lovers Lane and, after the streets were paved, divided them into lots for new brick homes. The north side of Lovers Lane was divided into fourteen lots, and building began there first.[150] Prior to this subdivision, the south side of the street already had three privately built homes not related to the company. Lovers Lane now intersects Cleveland Street. Its seclusion is a thing of the past.

Lowe Street

This street was named for Liberty County sheriff Pat Christian Lowe, who was born on June 28, 1895, to George Thomas and Pearl Donnella Hare Lowe. He was raised with seven siblings at Tarkington Prairie, where his father was a farmer. Pat and his brother Tom operated a store during World War I before moving to Orangefield. There they owned rental houses and operated a general store.

Later, Pat Lowe moved to Daisetta, Texas, where he worked for Humble Oil Company until 1922. Prior to 1920, he met and married Delia Berry. The couple had five children: Eunice; Buelah; Clarice, who went by "Babe"; Pat, who was called "PC"; and Vernon. In 1924, Pat and Delia moved to South Liberty and opened another store. Business was good because the first oil well came in at that time, and Liberty was joining in the oil boom. Sadly, on August 27, 1920, Delia and baby Betty died during childbirth.

Pat Lowe. *Courtesy of Lynne Lowe Harding.*

In 1930, Lowe was elected to the office of Liberty County sheriff. He said, "I ran because I'm just a country boy who wants to see things done right." For the next ten years, he served as sheriff, only giving up the election once during that time to Lockhart Hightower. During those ten years, he and his family lived in the home attached to the Liberty County Jail, where his second wife, Leona, was the chief cook for the inmates.

Lowe bought some "tourist courts" on the south side of Highway 90 in Dayton next to Frank's Cafe in 1945 and operated a sawmill as well. In 1947, he became a Phillips 66 jobber, purchasing fuel from refining companies. He also established Lowe Oil Company on the north side of Highway 90 at the top of Dayton Hill. There he built Lowe's Town House and Motel in 1961. The family continued to own and run the oil company for several years after his retirement. Lowe Street runs south to north through that business.[151]

Pat died on January 12, 1980, and is buried in Ryan Cemetery, close to Tarkington, Texas.

Luke Street

Luke Street is named for Luke Walker, who was born on September 23, 1884, in Frierson, Louisiana, to Mr. and Mrs. Ed Walker. Luke married Maud Dunlap, who grew up in Dayton and was the youngest of five children. She attended Dayton Public School under the administration of Mrs. Annie E. Colbert (see Colbert Street).

Luke Walker. *Courtesy of Dayton's Old School Museum.*

Luke is remembered fondly as a businessman who owned a barbecue restaurant frequented by many Dayton families, both black and white. He provided for the separation of the races, which was the custom of the times. He joined the Pleasant Hill Baptist Church under the pastorate of Reverend A.D. Jones. He was a member of Masonic Lodge No. 127, and his wife was a charter member of the Order of the Eastern Star.

Luke preceded his wife in death on September 18, 1962, and she followed on December 12, 1977. They are buried at Acie Cemetery in Dayton. The couple had no children but left behind many nieces, nephews and cousins.[152]

Main Street

The 1927 map of Dayton shows that present-day Main Street was originally named Second Street (First Street was present-day Church Street).[153] Dayton was recorded as an incorporated municipality on May 3, 1911,[154] according to a tiny article in the *Liberty Vindicator* dated February 17, 1911, that stated: "At the election holden at Dayton last Friday to determine whether or not that township should be incorporated, the question carried by a vote of: For incorporation 80; against incorporation 57."

For reasons unknown, another election was held on November 28, 1925, "to determine whether or not the town of Dayton, Liberty County, Texas, shall be incorporated, under provisions made in Chapter II, of the Revised Statues of the State of Texas of 1925."[155] The city election for Dayton was held on Saturday, February 6, 1926, for the election of officers who were as follows: W.S. Neel, mayor; R.N. Ford, J.L. Guice, C.M. Moller and C.F. Berry, aldermen; and A.S. Ratliff, marshal.[156]

By 1910, the town had 2,500 inhabitants and had a thriving business community. Many of the buildings in what is considered Dayton's historic downtown area were built early in the 1900s. A 1912 picture of Main Street shows that the Dayton Mercantile Building (#6–8), built by Ross Sterling,

Hauling rice up Main Street. *Courtesy of* Texas Illustrated Magazine.

Main Street with wagons and automobiles. *Courtesy of* Texas Illustrated Magazine.

Early Main Street scene. *Courtesy of* Texas Illustrated Magazine.

was standing. The Rio Movie Theater also existed by that time, shown in the same photo. The second location of Dayton State Bank (#24) retains the year 1919 above the entrance. Sterling also built the connecting buildings on the east of the street (#30–36) in the early 1920s.

Early pictures of Main Street show a dirt road that was extremely muddy after rains. Through the 1920s and late '30s, automobiles were few, with horses, buggies and wagons being the primary modes of transportation.

One business on Main, Kline's Grocery (#35 on the map), had a gas pump, but it also had cross rails so that horses could be tied. A shell surface paved the street until it was concrete paved and guttered in 1948–50 during the mayorship of Robert "Bobby" Harris.

Manor Street

Manor Street was developed for home sites in the late 1960s by Troy Wilson, who bought the land from the Dayton Future Farmers of America organization. It is so named because Heritage Manor Nursing Home, opened for residents about 1964, was already located on the property. The establishment is now known as Heritage Villa Nursing and Rehab Center.[157]

Marblehead Street

Because of two little girls, Marblehead Street is named for Ronald Ray "Mutt" Neuman. The story goes like this: Mutt's dad gave each of his seven children nicknames, and because Ronald had cotton-white hair as a child, he was nicknamed "Muttonhead," which was shortened after a while to Mutton. When he was in the fifth grade, it became Mutt, and that is what he has been called ever since. When Mutt was a child, many of Dayton's streets had no official names. They were known simply as where this or that family lived. Mutt's family lived on present Marblehead Street, which was a dirt path accessed from North Winfree Street by a short bridge spanning the ditch. The Bobbie Trousdale family were neighbors, and Mutt played with the two Trousdale girls. Instead of calling him Muttonhead, they thought it funny to call him Marblehead. When the Dayton City Council got around to naming the street back in the 1950s, the girls told the official who was

Mutt Neuman. *Courtesy of Mutt Neuman.*

out looking at the road that the name of their street was Marblehead. And that's how it got its name.

The property that later became home sites on the street was originally farmland and not located in the city limits. In the 1930s, E.B. "Lett" and Ada Gertrude Hooper Neuman, Mutt's parents, bought four acres on the corner of present Marblehead and North Winfree Streets and another acre from Mr. Angus Benton (see Benton Street), who farmed with mules. They were able to purchase Benton's acre after he became angry over the poor crop the land produced. He told Lett that he would sell the land for fifty dollars, so Mutt's mother, who saved dimes, made the downpayment on the land for ten dollars in dimes.

Esther Friedman Blonstein (see Esther Street) owned property on the same road that became very boggy after rains. The Haracek family, who lived on the road, had boys who were much older than Mutt. They would drive their dad's old car through the mud and made a trail all the way down to present Colbert Street. Other people eventually began using the trail in their vehicles and made a road out of it.

Mutt was born on November 5, 1945, in Liberty, the first of his siblings to be born in a hospital. The other six children—Jessie Eric, Gene Bert, E.B. Jr., Franky, Larry and Dora Ada—were born at the Neuman home, in which Mutt still lives and which includes all of the acreage his parents owned. Mutt's parents owned cows, horses, chickens, hogs and various other animals, and the children were quite involved in their care. Very interested in animals, Mutt appeared in his first rodeo when he was six years old as a calf rider. He was hooked. At the age of thirteen, Mutt began riding steers and horses, and in high school, with Mr. L.J. Chachere as his agriculture teacher, he began riding bulls. Mutt rodeoed all over the United States and in Guatemala. He rode his last bull at age forty-one at a rodeo in Chihuahua, Mexico. He is in the Louisiana Rodeo Hall of Fame.

Right after graduating from Dayton High School in 1964, Mutt opened Neuman's Gulf Service Station on U.S. Highway 90. He owned it for twenty-one years while also raising livestock. He raised and trained horses for twelve years, some of which raced at Vinton, Louisiana. Mutt owns his own rodeo arena on Highway 321 on seventeen acres, which he established after high school graduation and which has been the scene of weekend rodeos for a great many years. Mutt makes his facility, livestock, time and advice available to prospective bull riders and continues to produce bulls for the Professional Bull Riders Association rodeos. Mutt produced the rodeos at Pasadena's famous Gilley's every weekend from 1982 to 1989.

Mutt married his sweetheart Judy Robinson in 1969, and they had three children: Kody, Kail and Kacy.[158]

McBride Street

McBride Street is named for Martha A. "Lucy" McBride, referred to affectionately as "Mama Lucy" by her many friends. Lucy was born on January 18, 1889, and was married to Joe McBride. The couple had no children. She worked for the Ed Paul family (see Paul Street) for many years as a cook and was well known for her baking skills.

She was a faithful member of the Mt. Pleasant Baptist Church, serving as secretary for years. She also served as Sunday school superintendent, and nothing happened at the church that she wasn't a part of.[159] Beatrice Payne said that Mama Lucy absolutely lived by the golden rule: "Do unto others as you would have them do unto you."[160] Joann Paul related that Mama Lucy was a huge supporter of the community and the school, encouraging the children to study hard. She is very much missed by her community and friends.[161]

Lucy lived her last years with her brother in Houston. She passed away on June 17, 1973, and is buried at Acie Cemetery in Dayton.

Meadows Lane

Meadows Lane is part of a subdivision called the Meadows. On April 25, 2001, Boyd Arnold of Arnold Construction Company, Inc., purchased 7.25 acres of land on the corner of East Waring and Colbert Streets from F.M.

(Blackie) Graves. The land was platted into thirty-three lots by Norman Dykes, who was the engineer of the project.

Patsie Arnold named the subdivision the Meadows because, with the wildflowers and open area, it looked like a pretty meadow. She named the inside street Meadows Lane; Colbert Street was already named by the city. The first home was sold on December 7, 2002.[162]

Meremar Lane

Meremar Lane is named for Marcia Voytek Tillman and Meredith Voytek Stieler, daughters of Kenneth and Sandra Voytek, and is located in the Pecanwood Mobile Home Park.

The Voytek family moved to Dayton in 1976 when Kenneth accepted the position of principal at Stephen F. Austin Elementary, and Sandra became a fourth-grade reading teacher there. The Voytek girls were ages eleven and ten at that time. Kenneth wanted to acquire property for investment, so in 1978, he bought five acres on North Colbert Street paralleling the Linney and Acie Cemeteries with the intention of subdividing it into lots for home sites. He bought the property from Mrs. Nina Harrison and had a street built with utilities on the eighteen lots. The street was named when the deed was filed.

The early 1980s saw a recession that was brought on by high interest rates. This resulted in fewer homes being built, and since more people were purchasing mobile homes, the Voyteks decided to divide the lots into mobile home space rentals. The Pecan Wood Mobile Home Park opened in 1980 and was so named because there were large pecan trees on the property.

"Deciding on a name for the street was fairly easy," Sandra Voytek remembered. Several years earlier, the family had lived near Sam Rayborn and Toledo Bend Lakes and had acquired a bass boat. Since their girls, Marcia and Meredith, were small, it was a family project to name the boat. They decided on Meremar Sanken, a combination of letters of each of their names. The new Dayton street became Meremar Lane.

Marcia, a member of the National Honor Society and a Dazzler (the name of Dayton High School's drill/dance team), graduated from Dayton High School in 1983, receiving the DAR Award her senior year. She attended the University of Texas, graduating in 1986. She attended law school at St. Mary's in San Antonio and graduated with her law degree. Marcia married Rix Thomas "Tom" Tillman in 1991, and they have two children: Sarah

Left: Marcia Voytek. *Courtesy of Sandra Voytek. Right*: Meredith Voytek. *Courtesy Sandra Voytek.*

and Julia. At the time of this writing, Marica is a law partner in Darden, Fowler, and Creighton, LLP, in Conroe, Texas.

Meredith graduated from Dayton High School in 1984. She, too, was a member of the National Honor Society, was a Dazzler and received the DAR Award her senior year. She graduated from Texas A&M University in 1988 and became a certified public accountant. Meredith received her masters degree from Houston Baptist University in 1991. She worked in Houston for Marwick's Accounting Firm and then for the Enron Corporation. Meredith married Ricky Eggleston, her high school sweetheart, in 1990, and they had two children, Kathryn and Andrew. After Ricky's untimely death, she later met and married Justin Stieler of Kerrville, Texas. At the time of this writing, she is employed by Pathways Youth and Family Services as its director of operations.[163]

Merritt Street

William Merritt III. *Courtesy of the* Liberty Vindicator.

Merritt Street was originally called Avenue D[164] and is one of eleven roads renamed by the Dayton City Council in 1961 for Dayton servicemen killed in World War II. The street is named for William H. Merritt III, who was born November 15, 1908, and was the son of Charles E. and Augusta Merritt. William was named after his grandfather.

His obituary in the *Liberty Vindicator*, dated July 27, 1944, stated, "Corporal W.H. Merritt III, a radio repair man with the Ninth Air Force fighter squadron, was reported killed in an accident in England on July 1. He was an employee of Humble Oil and Refining Company on a lease near Lovell's Lake when he enlisted in the army two years ago. Surviving are his wife, Mildred who is one of the operators of M&M Beauty Shop in Liberty, two small sons: W.H. Merritt IV and Michael, his mother Mrs. Augusta Merritt of Dayton, his father, Charles E. Merritt of Logansport, La. and his grandmother, Mrs. W.H. Merritt II of Beaumont."[165]

He is buried at Sam Houston National Cemetery at Fort Sam Houston in San Antonio, Texas. According to his brother-in-law, Billy O'Neil, he was quite an easygoing man.[166]

Milo Street

This street is named for two men—Milo Westel Ford Sr. (called Milo) and Milo Westel Ford Jr. (called M.W.)—and was so named by John and Jessica Ford Johnson when they developed the Fordland Estates subdivision in 2002. The subdivision is located off Ford Avenue on family land that the Johnsons bought from her father. Information about Milo Westel Ford Sr. can be found in the Ford Avenue section.

M.W. Ford Jr. has lived in Dayton his entire life but was born in Houston on May 26, 1918. He grew up attending the First United Methodist Church and at age twelve played the organ chimes every day at 5:00 p.m. He took piano lessons for eleven years from Mrs. Rebecca Friedman Miller (daughter of Louis and Annie Friedman).

As a high school freshman, M.W. began working at Dayton State Bank, first sweeping the floors on Saturdays and gradually assuming more duties. He worked at the bank every weekend all through high school, graduating from Dayton High School in 1936 with nineteen other class members and from Rice University in 1940. After college graduation, M.W. began working at the bank as teller but felt he needed to serve his country, so he enlisted in the U.S. Air Force in December 1941 and served until 1946, when he was discharged with the rank of captain.

M.W. returned to the job he loved at the bank but, three years later, found out he had contracted tuberculosis and spent the next

Top: Milo Westel Ford Sr. *Courtesy of Jessica Ford Johnson.*

Bottom: M.W. Ford Jr. *Courtesy of Jessica Ford Johnson.*

three years in the Veterans' Administration Hospital in Kerrville, Texas. On returning to Dayton, a friend introduced him to Dorothy Fay Russell, who was working at the Pure Oil Company in Beaumont. Dorothy's family had moved around a lot because of her father's job in the oil fields, but she was born in Huffman, Texas, in December 1922, with Dr. J.T. Tadlock from Dayton performing the delivery.

In 1946, M.W.'s father divided the family homestead into five lots and gave a lot to each of his children. M.W. and Dorothy built their home in 1956 on his inheritance, where they raised two daughters, Gina Fay and Jessica. M.W. had a great opportunity to move to Houston to further his banking career but decided he wanted to stay in Dayton because he knew the people and wanted to raise his family here. From teller, he moved up the ladder to assistant cashier, cashier, executive vice-president and president. He retired in 1983 after working at the bank for fifty years. M.W. still serves on the advisory board of directors as of this writing.

In the early 1940s, M.W. became organist at the First Methodist Church. He was a pianist, but the church needed an organist. So he volunteered to learn how to play it and served for fifty years in that capacity, turning over the reigns to his daughter Jessica when he was ninety years old. Jessica is one of two organists as of this writing.

M.W. served as mayor of Dayton for two years (1969–70). He became mayor as a result of a write-in campaign (no one was running for mayor). The city council passed a one-cent city sales tax during his tenure.

Another of M.W.'s accomplishments is painting. He worked at a museum while a student at Rice University and developed a love for art. He learned technique as he watched his aunt paint and later took lessons from Katy Breeden in Kenefick.

"I have had a very blessed life," M.W. said at his interview. Dayton has been indeed blessed to have him as a resident.[167]

Mockingbird Lane

This is one of the streets in the Linney Creek subdivision. It is not known why the Slovers chose Mockingbird for the street name. See Atascocita, Slover and Myra Lane sections for more information.

Moller Street

This street is named for Charles Milton and Laura Alice White Moller, who owned the land where the street is located. Charles was born on August 5, 1882, in Texas and had at least seven siblings who were named in his 1943 obituary in the *Liberty Vindicator.*[168] During World War I, he was living in Harris County, receiving his draft registration card there during the year 1917–18.[169]

Laura Alice White was born on March 26, 1887, to parents Tillman Bailey White Jr. and Alice White. By the census of 1900, there were six children in the White household, including Laura. Her father was a farmer, and the family lived in Brazos, Texas.

Charles married Laura White prior to moving to Dayton, where they were living by 1920 as evidenced in the U.S. census of that year. No children were listed, but Laura's parents were part of the household at that time.[170]

Charles was very active in civic affairs. He was elected to the first group of aldermen to serve the newly incorporated city of Dayton. He took his oath of office on February 19, 1926.[171] He served on the Committee on Streets along with C.F. Berry and R.N. Ford. He was also appointed to the Committee on Sanitation with T.H. Shaw and J.L. Guice. He resigned his office on November 28, 1928.[172]

Moller's occupation had been as a dairyman, as evidenced in his obituary.[173] The Mollers were members of the First United Methodist Church, where Charles served as a trustee in 1925. The church records show that he was involved in the purchase of a tract of land for the new church building that was built in 1942–43.[174]

Charles Moller passed away on July 28, 1943, at the age of sixty. Laura died on February 2, 1977, and both are buried at Linney Cemetery in Dayton.

Myra Lane

Myra Lane is named for Myra Slover and is located in the Linney Creek subdivision. Myra and her husband, Roy, owned and subdivided the lots and named the streets in the late 1960s or early '70s. Myra Kelly was born on January 13, 1913, to George and Molly Kathleen Addkinson Kelly. She married J. Roy Slover (see Slover Street) on July 4, 1930, in Oklahoma, and the two of them came to Texas to live.

Myra Slover. *Courtesy of First Baptist Church, Liberty.*

In an interview with Mr. Ted Boyer, who as a young man worked part time for the Slovers, he said that Myra was Roy's right hand. Roy valued her opinion greatly and consulted her before making many decisions concerning investments. Myra owned and operated a flower shop in Liberty for several years and was a member of the Garden Club. She and her husband were faithful members of the First Baptist Church in Liberty.

Boyer said he has fond memories of Mrs. Slover and had great respect for her. He recalled the time he and his wife, Marjolaine, drove the Slovers to the Rio Grande Valley. Roy wasn't comfortable driving long distances due to an automobile accident that had caused him to lose sight in one eye, so he would ask Boyer to drive him different places. Myra and Roy loved to sing, and they sang in the car all the way to the Valley. Boyer would also drive them to the Houston Club, which they greatly enjoyed, as Mr. Slover got a lot of business from people he would meet there.

Myra was in the office of their Tri County Lumber Company much of the time, and upon Roy's death, she took over the reins of the businesses they owned. Boyer describes her as very attractive with good business sense. Because they had no children, Myra deeded the apartments Roy built in Austin to the Southwestern Baptist Theological Seminary upon her death. She also bequeathed part of their estate to the First Baptist Church in Liberty.[175]

Myra Slover died on December 16, 1996, and is buried in Fairlawn Cemetery in Liberty.

N–Z

Nancy Street

Nancy Street is named for Nancy Roberts, who lived in a house on that street. She was born on October 31, 1879. She was married, but the only information found by the author was that her husband's last name was Roberts and the couple had no children. It is believed that she made her living working as a domestic. Nancy was a member of St. Paul AME Church on State Highway 321. She died on January 17, 1961, and is buried at Acie Cemetery.[176]

Nelton Street

This street was originally named Cross Avenue and later called Belton.[177] It was renamed by Carl Truett Norcross, known as Truett, in honor of his mother and father. Truett had property on the corner of South Main and East Houston Streets. The present Nelton Street was the north boundary of his property. Several years prior to 1999, he petitioned Dayton City Council to name what was then a little dirt road "Nelton Street." The council granted his request.

Later, in a letter he wrote to Clarence Martin, who was affiliated with First Liberty National Bank, dated May 8, 1999, he explained, "Nelton is a

Milton and Nellie Norcross. *Courtesy of Zoe Norcross.*

juxtaposition of the first half of my Mother's name, Nellie, and the last half of my Dad's name, Milton." Another affiliate with the bank, Paul J. Henry, wrote back to Truett on May 12, 1999, saying, "We are in the process of paving Nelton Street. I think after we are complete, Nelton Street will be a great tribute to your Father and Mother."

Milton Frank Norcross was born on June 16, 1904, in China, Jefferson County, Texas, to Frank and Lucy Tilton Norcross (see Norcross Lane). In 1911, when Milton was seven years old, the family moved to Dayton. There he grew up with two younger brothers, Walter and Carl, living on property divided by the street that now bears the Norcross name.

Nellie Julia Wright was born on February 15, 1902, in Newton County, Texas to Valentine and Julia Ann Sheppard Wright. Milton and Nellie married on April 12, 1930, in Dayton and had two children: Carl Truett, known as Truett, born in 1931, and Irma Nell Norcross Whittington, known as Nell, born in 1935.

Milton worked for years for Liberty County running a maintainer, a piece of road construction equipment. Both were members of the First United Methodist Church of Dayton. Milton died on June 26, 1976, at age seventy-two. Nellie died on September 8, 1988. Both are buried at Linney Cemetery.[178]

Daughter Nell Whittington wrote of her parents:

> *Mother came from a very large family and had numerous relatives. She was a very giving Christian lady and a fantastic cook. At the age of 65, she opened a neighborhood grocery, Norcross Grocery, and operated it for several years. Daddy did the banking and some of the ordering. Truett bought them out and still owned the store at the time of his death in 2005, though it was leased out. The store was located on West Clayton* [FM 1960] *in Dayton. Since Truett's death, his children have sold the store location and it is no longer a grocery.*[179]

Granddaughter Zoe Norcross wrote of her grandparents:

> *Big Daddy, as his grandkids called him, loved listening to the Astros and watching HeeHaw. He smoked Roi-Tan cigars. He was very foreboding and gruff to all of us kids but we loved him dearly! He loved buttermilk and cornbread. He was just one of the original "good ol' boys." When I was about ten or so, he and Grandma bought the store. The stock room in back had a cot so Big Daddy could take his nap.*
>
> *In 1976, he was diagnosed with lung cancer. While at MDAnderson, all five of us grand kids went to visit him. We sat on the empty bed next to his and Grandma said, "Look there, all your grand kids came to visit you!" He leaned forward and counted, "1, 2, 3, 4, 5. Yep, they're all here." He was a dear man.*
>
> *My grandmother was the best cook ever. She taught me how to make gravy. She got me hooked on coffee-milk. She made her own fig preserves and chow-chow. She was a tiny woman who didn't ever wear slacks until I was about 12 or so…then she wore them constantly and only wore a dress to church. She made aprons out of feed sacks.*[180]

Norcross Lane

Norcross Lane was named after Amos Franklin and Lucy Virginia Tilton Norcross. They moved to Dayton in 1911 and purchased land that lay on both sides of the road that now bears their name: forty acres on the south side and five acres on the north side, which was planted as a pecan orchard.

Amos and Lucy Norcross. *Courtesy of Nell Norcross Whittington.*

Amos Franklin "Frank" Norcross was born on September 22, 1879, in Austin County, Texas, to parents George W. and Mary Emeline Shaver Norcross. Frank was baptized in 1882, as recorded in the family Bible. The 1900 U.S. census showed that Frank, age twenty and single, was living with his brother T.W. Norcross in Burleson, Texas, and worked as a farm laborer.[181] Two years later, he married Lucy Virginia Tilton on November 12 in Chambers County. The marriage license was issued from Jefferson County, Texas, and the marriage is recorded there. The ceremony was performed by a Chambers County justice of the peace.

Lucy Tilton was born on November 10, 1882, in Chambers County to John Milton and Effie Sophia Brashear Tilton. She was baptized on June 25, 1885, in Chambers County, as recorded in the Tilton family Bible. Two years after their marriage, the couple had their first child, Milton Frank Norcross, who was born on June 16, 1904, in China, Jefferson County, Texas. The 1910 U.S. census showed the family still residing there, and Frank's occupation was listed as a farmer on a truck farm.[182] The Norcross family had increased by one, with another son, Walter Roscoe Norcross, born on July 1, 1908.

The Norcross family made the move to Dayton in 1911, and Frank received his World War I draft registration card during the year 1917–18 in Liberty County.[183] For a short time, the family resided at Goose Creek in Harris County, living there at the time of the 1920 U.S. census.[184] Three children were now part of the household, with a third son, Carl Alton, born October 6, 1914. Frank continued farming, and the family belonged to the Methodist church.

Frank passed away on June 5, 1951, in Dayton. Lucy died on March 9, 1970, and both are buried at Linney Cemetery in Dayton.

Granddaughter Nell Whittington wrote the following account about her grandparents:

> *Pa Pa and Ma Ma bought land on a country lane outside Dayton in 1911 and lived there until his death in 1951 except for a short period in Goose Creek. This was almost a magical place for a child with ponds full of hybrid water lilies, a concrete horse trough with numerous huge goldfish, large pecan trees, and flowers everywhere. One of the highlights of my summer was helping Pa Pa catch the fish in the trough and put them in a #3 wash tub while the trough was cleaned. The lane was to become known as Norcross Lane and is to this day. From the point where Pa Pa's land began, huge cedar trees lined the road on the south side and a pecan orchard on the north, all the way up to the house. A huge sweet gum tree stood in front of the house, with the lane curving around one side of it and the driveway on the other side. A grapefruit tree grew in a sheltered area at the rear of the house. My grandparents were truck farmers and were well known in the community. Merchants in town kept vases handy to receive the flower bouquets that were cut almost daily in season from their yard and delivered to them.*[185]

Oak Street

Oak Street was so named because there were many large oak trees on this property. Many of the trees were cut down in 2010 and 2011, some due to the damage sustained by Hurricane Ike in 2009. This was one of four streets developed beginning in 1957 in the Dayton Heights subdivision by the Trinity Development Company. Bucky Buchanan headed the company, which was also owned by Bobby Harris and Joe Harris, prominent businessmen in Dayton; Bobby Roberts, vice-president of the Liberty National Bank; and possibly Marvin Henry, the surveyor for the development. The other streets laid out by the company were Cypress (now Lawrence), Pine and Willow.[186]

Park Place

David Parker. *Courtesy of David Parker.*

Park Place was named for David Allen Parker. He, along with Randy West, owned a total of forty-two acres that they subdivided into lots and sold in 1977. This subdivision became two streets, Park Place and Westwood.

David Parker was born on July 19, 1945, to Robert and Lillian Payne Parker at Liberty Catholic Hospital. He grew up in Dayton with two brothers, Douglas and Doak. David graduated from Dayton High School in 1963 and from Baylor University in 1969.

Following college graduation, David married Susan Daniel of Liberty on March 28, 1970. The couple had three children: Daniel Martin, Mollie Suellen and Will Daniel. They bought and lovingly restored the oldest house in Liberty, attaching to it a larger, newly built home.

David's careers included savings and loan officer; real estate broker, owning Town & Country Realty; home builder; and land developer. He enjoys collecting antiques, is a Christian and is a member of the Dayton Rotary Club and the Dayton Historical Society, where he regularly gives programs relating to Dayton's history. David is an avid historian, especially interested in Dayton's history as well as family history. In 2012, David made a major contribution to the Dayton Historical Society in memory of his parents, which resulted in the addition of a lovely building to the Old School Museum. It is known as the Robert and Lillian Parker Meeting Room.

As a project of the Dayton Historical Society, David hopes to collect many oral histories from people in the community in order to preserve the stories and memories of the residents of Dayton.[187]

Paul Street

Paul Street is named for Edward "Ed" Paul and is located in the area north of Dayton known as the Old French Settlement. Born in Dayton in 1874 to Dave and Clare Roberts Paul, Ed was raised with a sister named Harriett. Several other siblings died as children.

Ed bought twenty-four acres in the Old French Settlement in 1898. Before being renamed for the Creoles (people with a mixture of French and Spanish blood) who came from Louisiana, the land was called Tasso Country, so named by the Indians who had lived there. State Highway 321, constructed in 1936, ran through his property and divided his acreage to both sides of the road.

Ed was a well digger by trade, bringing in water wells for many people. He was also a farmer, raising corn, garden vegetables and sugar cane. People from all around brought their sugar cane to Paul to refine into syrup at his mill. He was a rancher, using the DP brand that came from his dad. At that time, the cattle could roam everywhere and brands were important identification. In the mid-1950s, the Stock Law was passed whereby people had to keep their cows fenced.

Ed Paul. *Courtesy of Joann Paul.*

Ed married Pearl Cabello (born in 1877), who became well known for her wonderful cornbread. They had seven children: Audry, Otto, Sidney, Buck, Aggie, Cato and Ona. Ed was active in civic affairs and died in 1952 after being run over while crossing Highway 321. He was eighty-three years old and is buried at Acie Cemetery. Pearl died at age forty in 1920 and is also buried at Acie. Many of their descendants still reside in Dayton.[188]

Pecan Street

A pecan orchard located near the Linney Creek subdivision, in which this street is found, is the reason for the street's name. See Atascocita, Slover Street and Myra Lane sections for more information.

Pine Place

Pine Place subdivision was developed by David Allen Parker (see Park Place section) beginning on July 21, 1986. Approximately six acres were divided into twenty lots, and the houses were built to meet the requirements of Farmers Home Administration loan specifications. The name was chosen because of the many pine trees on the lots.[189]

Pine Street

Pine Street, subdivided by the Trinity Development Company, was part of the Dayton Heights subdivision and was so named because of the numerous pine trees located on this property. See Oak Street section for more information.

Prater Street

Prater Street is named for the family of Dennis and Melinda Prater Sr., who owned the land on which the street is located. One of their descendants, Sherial Lawson, believes that the land was previously owned by Dennis's father, but no information can be found about him.[190]

Dennis was born in Texas in 1830, and Melinda was born in Texas in 1845. They are found in the 1870 Precinct 4 (now Dayton) U.S. census, with Dennis at age forty and Melinda age thirty-five. They had two children: Warner, age illegible, and Alice, age two. Dennis's occupation was listed as farming, and Melinda's was housekeeping.

Dennis and Melinda's son, Warner, was born on January 8, 1860, and their daughter, Alice, in January 1868. The 1880 census showed Dennis listed incorrectly as sixty years old, but Melinda was not listed as part of the household. Living with Dennis was his son, Warner; Warner's wife, Harriett; and their one-year-old daughter, Matilda. Also in the household was Dennis's daughter, Alice, listed as age fourteen but who would have been twelve.

Dennis owned a forty-acre tract that was evenly divided between his children, Warner and Alice, presumably at his death.

Warner and Harriet had eight children: Robert (born 1882), Dennis B. (born 1885), Mack (born 1887), Bennie (born 1890), Alford (born 1891), Oldis (born 1893), Beatrice (born 1897) and Joseph (born 1899). In the 1900 census, Warner was living in Fort Bend, Texas, listed as married sixteen years, while Harriet was living with the children in Dayton, also listed as married.

The 1910 census showed Warner as a boarder of Alabama Cole. This was also listed as his residence in 1930. The 1910 census showed Harriet as the wife of James Best, with children Johnnie, Bennie, Archie, Oldis, Beatrice and Clarence Gray living with them. Her occupation was home laundress. By 1920, the Best household included children Beatrice, Archie and Clarence Gray. James Best was a cook in a restaurant, and no occupation was listed for Harriet.

Dennis's daughter, Alice, married Brayboy Lawson (1851–1941) on December 27, 1887, in Liberty County. They had ten children: Melinda (1889–1934), Spencer (1890–1964), Birdie (1891–1983), Clara (1892–1971), Crockett Wright (1893–1932), Edna Ida (1894–1979), Richard (1897–1974), Warner (1899–1988), Blanch (1903–1983) and Eugene (1905–1929).[191]

Alice died on May 25, 1905, at the age of thirty-five. Alice's great-granddaughter Annette Lockett said that the cemetery where Alice is buried is, for the most part, lost.[192] Alice's brother, Warner, passed away on June 5, 1952, and is buried at Acie Cemetery in Dayton. The descendants of Warner and Alice, many of whom reside in Dayton, have continued to inherit and divide the land handed down to them.

Pruitt Street

Pruitt Street is named for the Edmund Pruett family (spelled Pruett, Pruitt and Prewitt in various places). On the gravestone at the French Cemetery in Dayton, the name is Pruett. When the street was platted, someone spelled the name incorrectly as Pruitt.

Edmund Pruett was the son of Beasley Pruett Jr. and his wife, Rebecca Linney, who was the daughter of Michael and Rebecca Weeks Linney (see Linney Street). Edmund, born on March 22, 1846, in Dayton, known then as West Liberty, had seven siblings who lived past childhood: Riley Cynthia (1848–1886), William P. (1851–1881), Colbert Fullman (1854–1905), James (1864–1882), Lucy (1860–1902), Henry (1869–1945) and Price (1871–1941).

Edmund was given a public school education of a limited nature and grew up amid rural surroundings, being trained in the duties of the home farm. He was fifteen years of age when, in August 1861, he entered the Civil War and joined Company F, Fifth Texas Regiment, under Colonel Bryant, which formed a part of Hood's Brigade and went directly to Virginia. Edmund was disabled early on and was discharged after nine months without taking part in any engagement. He then returned to his home, where he remained until 1864, and that year joined Company F, of Colonel Spaight's Regiment of the Texas Infantry, with which he served along the coast until his regiment was disbanded at the close of the war.

After the completion of his military service, Edmund engaged in the stock business at his old home. He had made no money prior to the war and had none afterward with which to begin business. The nineteen-year-old really got his start by working for wages as a farmer and also by cropping for himself. He worked for as little as $0.50 per day and invested his small savings in cattle, horses and land, paying at that time about $2.50 a head for cattle and about $5.00 a head for horses. For land, he paid from $0.50 to $1.00 an acre.

Edmund purchased his first land from the Thomas J. Haggerty heirs in the Haggerty survey. During the panicky conditions of 1886–88, Edmund weathered the storm but, for three years, sold nothing. When he finally did find a profitable market, his ranch was covered with stock. Before the coming of the Southern Pacific Railroad, he drove his stock to Louisiana and peddled the cattle to the planters. He accumulated about 11,300 acres. He introduced Brahman cattle into his herd and successfully crossed them with native stock.

Edmund served his county as a member of the Board of Commissioners for eight years. All matters of civic virtue and civic pride were of interest to him, and his cooperation was given to many measures that were directly beneficial to the city of Dayton and the surrounding country in the line of its material, intellectual and moral progress.

Edmund was married first in April 1866 to Lucinda Abshier, daughter of Asa Abshier, who came to Texas from Louisiana. Lucinda died in May

1889, leaving no children. He then married in March 1890 to Minnie Day, daughter of William Day, who was a resident of Memphis, Tennessee. Of this union, there was a son, Edmund Day Pruett, who was born and raised in Dayton and engaged in the cattle business with his father. Edmund Day Pruett married Ethel Littler.[193]

Edmund Pruett died on May 2, 1918. Minnie Day Pruett, who was born on November 3, 1866, died on June 15, 1937. Lucinda Abshier, Edmund's first wife, was born on April 12, 1843. All three are buried at French Cemetery in Dayton.[194]

Ranchwood

This is one of the streets in the Linney Creek subdivision. It is not known why the Slovers chose Ranchwood for the street name. See Atascocita, Slover Street and Myra Lane sections for more information.

River Oaks

This street was named after the affluent subdivision in Houston with the same name. The name was chosen because the subdivision Suburban Acres was built with nice homes on large lots. Development began in 1964 by the children of W.T. and Allene Jamison (see Jamison Street section).[195]

Ross Street

This street is named for Ross Shaw Sterling, who never lived in Dayton but had a significant role in its development. Sterling was born in Anahuac, Texas, in February 1875 to Benjamin Franklin and Jane Bryan Sterling. He received little formal education and worked as a farmer until opening a feed store at Sour Lake in 1903. This was a great success, and he later purchased a number of small banks, including one in Dayton (Dayton State Bank). He was a charter founder of the Dayton Lumber Company in 1905, and when the original ownership went bankrupt in 1912, he took over the mill.

Ross Sterling. *Courtesy of Texas State Library & Archives Commission.*

Sterling also invested in the oil industry and, in 1910, started a new venture that developed into the Humble Oil and Refining Company. In 1917, he chartered and built the Dayton–Goose Creek Railroad (see Goosecreek Street section) for moving his freight and petroleum products to his Humble refinery in Baytown. He sold this rail line to Southern Pacific in 1926. In 1925, he sold Humble Oil and used the money to invest in real estate in the Houston area. He also purchased the *Houston Dispatch* (1925) and the *Houston Post* (1926).

A member of the Democratic Party, Sterling was elected governor of Texas and took office on January 20, 1931. He was defeated in his second bid for governor as the result of his role in a dispute between the major oil production companies and independent oil producers.

Sterling returned to the oil industry after losing his post as governor. He established Sterling Oil and Refining Company in 1933. He was also president of the R.S. Sterling Investment Company and the American Maid Flour Mills. He was chairman of the Houston National Bank.

Sterling married Maud Abbie Gage on October 10, 1898, and they became the parents of five children. Among his philanthropies was the gift of his La Porte home to the Houston Optimist Club for a boys' home; establishment of a boys' camp in memory of Ross Sterling Jr., who died in 1924; and the contribution of $100,000 to Texas Christian University. He was a Free Mason.

Ross Shaw Sterling died in Fort Worth on March 25, 1949, and is buried at Glenwood Cemetery in Houston.[196] Maud died on March 7, 1963, and is also buried at Glenwood Cemetery.

Sawmill Road

Sawmill Road was named sometime after World War II, according to Robert "Bobby" Harris. It received its name because of its proximity to a steam-powered sawmill built by J.D. Harris Jr. (Bobby's father) between 1930 and 1936 on the southern end of Waco Street. It sat back from the east side of the road a bit and was just north of the Southern Pacific Railroad (which followed the present railroad tracks that run east–west through Dayton). The sawmill was also on the west side of the old Trinity Valley and Northern tracks (the tracks that run to Baytown).

Sawmill Road was never the site of a sawmill itself.[197]

Seaberg Industrial Road

Seaberg Industrial Road is named for Roy Alfred Seaberg Sr., a prominent Dayton rice farmer who built this road leading to the rice dryer that he also constructed.

Roy was born on September 24, 1913, in Dayton to Charles Frederick and Sophia Victoria Johnson Seaberg. He grew up with brothers Charles Ivan, called Ivan, and Herbert Frederick, who was known as Uncle Dutch. Their sister, Dorothy, died at a very young age. Roy's family lived in the Stilson community, where he resided until 1966, when he and his wife built a house on South Church Street.

In their youth, Roy and his brothers worked on their father's farm, their father being one of the first rice farmers in Dayton. Charles Frederick and Sophia were Swedish immigrants who moved to Dayton from Iowa after seeing an advertisement for good farmland placed by a land developer. Charles Frederick Seaberg began farming rice around Dayton about 1906. Roy related that in those early days, they used horse-drawn wagons, and his mother cooked two meals a day for forty workers on a wood-burning stove with only one helper. Weekly, a wagon was sent to Houston to get sacks of flour, sugar and other supplies.

Their Swedish parents wouldn't allow Roy, Ivan or Dutch to speak Swedish, only English, knowing that it was important to their futures. Roy graduated from Dayton High School in 1931. Roy and Dutch stayed home after high school graduation and worked to help their brother Ivan go to college. Both Roy and Dutch continued in the rice farming business.

Roy Seaberg. *Courtesy of Susan Seaberg.*

Roy Seaberg met Juanita Addington in Dayton, where her family had moved after her high school graduation. Juanita was born on August 12, 1914, in Mineral Wells, Texas, and her father, Curtis Addington, worked for Sinclair Oil. Her family lived in many towns, including Teague, Mexia, Mineral Wells, Wichita Falls and Archer City. She worked as a telephone operator in Dayton prior to marrying Roy. They married on December 7, 1937, and raised three children: Roy Alfred Jr., Curtis "Allen" Addington and Kenneth Robert "Bob." Juanita was a homemaker, keeping the busy household running. She was also well read and had a lot of common sense.

Roy was a lifelong rice and soybean farmer and cattleman. The Seabergs' daughter-in-law Susan, who is married to Bob, described her father-in-law as a devoted husband, a role model father who was faithful to his church and God and a workaholic who was always seeking a better way to farm. He was fixated on weather conditions and was very involved in his community. She said, "He was a quiet, humble man, kind, and always the gentleman."

Roy started Seaberg Rice, Inc., and was an active member of First United Methodist Church. He served on the American Rice Growers Association Board of Directors, the Dayton ISD Board of Trustees, the San Jacinto Methodist Hospital Board of Directors, American Rice Growers Co-op Association of Dayton Board, the Blue Ribbon Rice Mill Board, the Production National Life Insurance Board, the Texas Rice Council Board, the Texas Rice Improvement Association Board, the Federal Land Bank of Houston Board, the Federal Land Bank of Dayton Board and the Dayton State Bank Board.

He was also a member of the Magnolia Cemetery Association. He and his father purchased and donated the land for the cemetery in the 1940s. When their sons married, Roy and Juanita were proud to have their three daughters-in-law in the family. In their elder years, they traveled quite a bit with friends. Roy always wanted to go to Russia but said they didn't start traveling early enough, and too soon, old age infirmities put a stop to the travels. Their last years were spent surrounded by family, including their eight grandchildren. Roy enjoyed deer hunting and dabbling in the oil business.

Roy died on March 6, 2005, and Juanita died on November 14, 2007. Both are buried at Magnolia Park Cemetery in Dayton.

Roy's family has only good memories of their patriarch: he always picked up the check when the family or friends went out to dinner; he was at times all business and at other times warm and very kind; he always tried to do the right thing whatever the situation; he was so proud that all three of his sons graduated from college, as it had been a goal for him and Juanita; and he was always a gentleman, opening doors for ladies and removing his hat inside. He left a legacy for his family, full of wonderful memories.[198]

Seekamp Street

Seekamp Street was first named Candor and later Avenue A.[199] It is one of eleven streets renamed in 1961 by the Dayton City Council for Dayton servicemen killed in World War II. The street is named for Vernon H. Seekamp, the son of Hugo and Millie Seekamp. Although Vernon never actually lived in Dayton, he was married to a local girl—LaVergne Whittle of Eastgate Community.

Vernon Seekamp. *Courtesy of Candace Seekamp Colby.*

Seekamp was born on April 7, 1917, and grew up in Victoria, Texas, with two sisters: Fern Seekamp Huddler and Marie Seekamp Dillon. After graduating from Victoria High School in 1933, he was representative and distributor of publications for the Curtis Publishing Company in Beaumont, Texas. While on the campus of Lamar College (now Lamar University), Vernon met LaVergne, who was attending school there. He asked her for a date, and they later married about 1938.[200]

Vernon joined the air force in January 1943 because he wanted to be a fighter pilot. He graduated from Aloe Army Air Field on January 7, 1944, where he was awarded the Aerial Gunnery Medal. He served as formation instructor at Camp Springs Army Air Base in Washington, D.C.

Seekamp, a P-47 pilot, went overseas in February 1945 and was awarded the Air Medal with three Oak Leaf Clusters and Presidential Unit Citation while with the First Tactical Air Force in France. After V-E Day, he was transferred to the Ninth Air Force in Germany. He was killed over Germany on July 10, 1945, as a result of an airplane crash while on a routine flight. He left behind his wife, LaVergne, and a one-month-old baby daughter, Candace "Candy" Seekamp (later Candace Colby). He died at the age of twenty-eight.[201]

Shanks Street

Shanks Street is named for the Shanks family, who for generations has owned the land where the street is located. Prior to the time when the name was given to the road, the land was owned by the Gosse family. In the 1830s, George (1825–1900) and Mary Elizabeth Schneider Gosse (1823–1885) immigrated to Texas from France. They married the day before they stepped on the boat that brought them here. They bought several parcels of land in what was called West Liberty at the time and today is known as Dayton.

This was a tumultuous time in Texas, as delegates were voting for independence from Mexico and the Battle of the Alamo had been fought. People received the news that Santa Anna's soldiers were marching in this direction, and they began fleeing the area in an episode that has come to be called the Texas Runaway Scrape. George gathered his family (wife, Mary Elizabeth, and two daughters, Eugenia and Mary Hortence) and left their home. After the Battle of San Jacinto and when the danger had passed, they returned. The Gosses farmed and raised cattle. George and Mary Elizabeth are buried at Linney Cemetery in Dayton.

Mary Hortence Gosse met a gentleman named Granville Marion Shanks (1857–1939) from Missouri, who came to West Liberty as an engineer for the Southern Pacific Railroad. This system came into being in 1886 when the Texas and New Orleans Railroad merged with the Louisiana and Western Railroad line. Mary and Granville married and settled on the

Dick Shanks. *Courtesy of Kathryn Shanks Martin.*

Gosse land, raising four children: Francis Marion, Richard "Dick" Earl, Louise Gosse McHugh and Ida Gosse Lewis.

Granville Shanks became an attorney and also farmed and raised livestock. Grandaughter Kathryn Shanks Martin related a story told to her by her grandmother Mary Hortence of feeding the children of Indians who would occasionally travel through the area. Granville and Mary are also buried in the Linney Cemetery.

The family land was passed to the Shankses' children, and Dick Shanks (1901–1996) and Francis Marion Shanks continued to live there through their adult years. Dick resided on the corner of Ford Avenue and Shanks Avenue. The home still belongs to the family. Their sister Ida moved back to Dayton in later years and also lived there. Dick and his siblings attended school at the Old School (restored by the Dayton Historical Society as a museum) and also at the "new" school, which was located in the block skirted by Houston and present-day Highway 90 in front and back and Cleveland Street and present-day Main Street at its sides. As was common in those days, Dick completed the eighth or ninth grade.

Dick married Thelma Lee Fingleman (1903–1981), and they had two children: Kathryn and Granville Marion, named after his grandfather. Dick worked for the Texaco Oil Company, which had a pumping station south of his home on the Munson League land. He and his brother Francis farmed and also ran cattle. Lester Ray Wisegerber described Dick Shanks as a very nice man who didn't mind young people gathering on his property to picnic and race horses. Shanks' Hill was the place for an annual event called "Kids' Day," which was celebrated by Dayton High School's senior students each year. They dressed as children and had a day of picnicking and fun.

Another very popular event that some called the Kentucky Derby of Dayton took place every Sunday afternoon at Shanks' Hill. Local people who owned horses would gather to race them, to the delight of many spectators. Two big racers were Seth Kay and Chester Holbrook (see Chester Street). A little betting may have also taken place.[202] Dick and Thelma are buried at Linney Cemetery.

The next generation to live on Shanks family land was Kathryn Shanks, born in 1927. She graduated from Dayton High School in 1944 and married a local boy, Bob Martin (1927–2000). After Bob joined the military, they left Dayton and lived wherever his job took them. He also worked for the Shell Oil Exploration Company, which took them various places to live. They returned to Dayton in 1957 to raise their two children: Marion Martin Stampley, who graduated from Dayton High School in 1964, and Robert Earl, who graduated in 1965. Bob opened an insurance agency with Bob Jamison, and Kathryn worked part time in the business. After being a homemaker for many years, she worked for lawyers Zeke Zbranek and Neal Iverson, as well as for a lawyer in Houston. She worked for the Liberty County sheriff's department in administration, retiring from that position. As of this writing, she continues to work part time for the Dayton Police Department as a computer inputer.[203]

Sherwood Drive

This was the first street developed by Bobby and Joe Harris when they bought the land for the Sherwood subdivision in 1955. They briefly considered naming the subdivision Linney Hill but decided on Sherwood, after the affluent Memorial area of Houston.[204] See Little John section for more information.

Skylark

This street is located in the Suburban Acres subdivision, work on which began in 1964 by the children of W.T. and Allene Jamison (see Jamison Street). This area was open prairie land and was so named because birds were easily seen flying in the sky. The Jamisons liked the way the name sounded.[205]

Slover Drive

This was the first street developed in the Linney Creek subdivision and was named for James Roy Slover, owner and subdivider. Although they never lived on the property, Roy and Myra Slover had a house there that they referred to as the creek house because of its proximity to Linney Creek. Slover had a dam built on Linney Creek and used the water to irrigate a large garden that was maintained on the property by Ted Boyer. Slover bought a mule for Boyer to use to do the plowing.

Roy was born on June 24, 1906, in Wayne County, Illinois, and moved to Oklahoma with his parents, William Author and Mary Elizabeth Garrison Slover. He married Myra Kelly on July 4, 1930, in Oklahoma. Roy and Myra came to Texas from Yale, Oklahoma, located outside Stillwater. As a young man, he worked for Sun Oil Company and was able to use that connection to help in later business ventures. The Slovers lived in Anahuac for a time before moving to the hill country for three or four years. He bought a ranch in Junction and a 250-acre ranch in Blanco, living in both before moving to Liberty. Roy and Myra Slover never resided in Dayton, but Roy was an influential man in Liberty County, owning businesses in Liberty and land in Dayton.

According to Boyer, a part-time employee, business associate and friend of the Slovers, Roy was quite a businessman and watched for investment opportunities. He built many apartments in Austin close to the University of Texas campus. He owned Tri County Lumber Company as well as a concrete and oil field mud business and had a home construction business, all in Liberty. Slover subdivided the lots and built many of the homes in the Treetop Terrace subdivision in Liberty.

Roy Slover. *Courtesy of the* Liberty Vindicator.

Boyer said Slover was an honest businessman who believed in giving people the opportunity to invest in ventures. Mr. Slover would advise, and Boyer would invest a little in each venture. They invested in gas lift wells in Hardin and bought the St. Lawrence #1 oil well together at Barbers Hill. They bought a farm together in Nome in 1979 and raised soybeans for several years. In 1966, Boyer bought three acres from the Slovers and built his house in what would become the Linney Creek subdivision. In the late 1960s or early '70s, Boyer helped the Slovers subdivide and sell the lots in the subdivision. All of the streets were laid out and named at the same time, with Slover Street being the first one with homes and the one on which Boyer's house was located.

Boyer fondly remembers Roy and the times they would hunt deer with the dogs (usually Australian shepherds) on the Linney Creek property, sometimes joined by District Judge Wheat, who was a good friend of Roy's. Two of Slover's favorite horses were named Buck and Rocket. Roy served as president of the chamber of commerce and was a member of the Liberty Rotary Club and Liberty Masonic Lodge, No. 48.

On a trip to Nome while calling on customers, Roy had an automobile accident and lost eyesight in one eye. He had a glass eye for the rest of his life.[206] Roy Slover died on November 1, 1986, at the age of eighty, and after his funeral service at the First Baptist Church with the Reverend Jerry Johnson officiating, a Masonic grave site service was held. He is buried in Liberty at Fairlawn Cemetery. (See also Myra Lane section.)

Smith Street

Smith Street was named in 1961 on the recommendation of Mayor James B. "Jim" Sterling Jr. in honor of Mamie Smith, a valued employee of his family for many years.[207] Mamie was born on May 29, 1887, in Texas, mostly likely in Dayton. She was first married to Will LaCour from Louisiana, and the couple had two sons, Carey (1905–1983) and Percy (1907–2006), who were born in Dayton. (See LaCour Street.)

According to the 1920 U.S. census, Mamie was married to Pleasant L. Smith and living in Dayton. Residing with them were her sons, Carey and Percy, and also Stella Smith, age twenty, presumably a daughter of Pleasant. Also in the household were Maydee Smith (age nine), daughter of Mamie and Pleasant, and Arthuella Smith (age four), possibly Stella's daughter. Mamie was found in the 1930 and 1940 census records, still living in Dayton and married to Pleasant Smith.[208]

From her granddaughter Annie Wingo it was learned that Mamie was head cook at Colbert School in the 1940s. She also worked for the

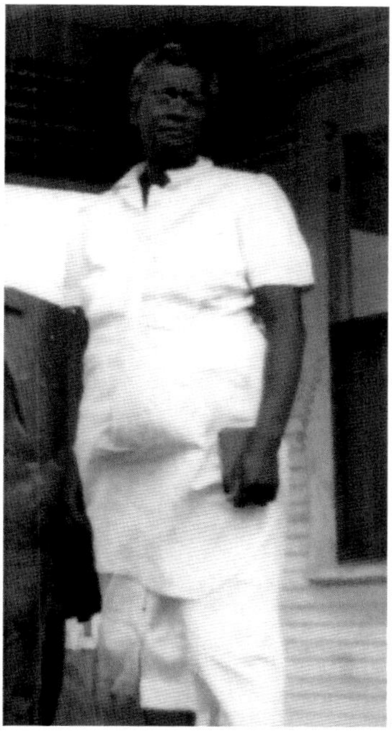

Mamie Smith. *Courtesy of Dayton's Old School Museum.*

James B. Sterling Sr. family as a cook for years.[209] Betty Sterling, wife of the late Jim Sterling, previously mentioned, said that Mamie was working for Jim's family when they married in 1948. She described Mamie as an absolutely wonderful lady, very dependable, honest and religious. When Jim and Betty had their first child, Jimmy, Mamie came and stayed with them to help out. She remained with the family through Jim's mother's illness and death; through the birth of the Sterlings' second child, Ben; and until Ben began school. At that time, she retired.[210] Mamie also helped Ruth Hensarling with her children when she was teaching school.[211]

Mamie was a faithful member of Pleasant Hill Baptist Church. She died on February 16, 1975, and is buried at Acie Cemetery in Dayton.

State Highway 146

State Highway 146 was designated as such about 1935 according to records at the Texas Department of Transportation's Liberty office. A portion of this highway runs south from its intersection with U.S. Highway 90 in Dayton. Prior to its current route from Dayton to Mont Belvieu, the section of road was a two-lane dirt road occasionally coated with oil to contain the dust. Longtime resident E.B. Neuman II said that the road did not follow the route it takes today:

> *In 1929–'30, it was a two-lane dirt road that ran to Barbers Hill* [Mont Belvieu] *starting about the same place as now where it turns left from U.S. Highway 90 going south. It ran parallel to the Goose Creek Railroad tracks for six miles, crossed the canal and turned right at Gum Island* [a large stand of gum trees]. *The path it followed is now County Road 479 where the American Rice Growers Company camp house is currently located.*

Highway 146 is pictured in this 1920s photo. This spot is next to today's Palms Memorial Cemetery. Visible is the Humble pump station with the home of Addy Graves in the background. *Courtesy of* Texas Illustrated Magazine.

> *The very narrow road then ran south, parallel to the railroad tracks all the way through the country until it turned left at Barbers Hill onto what is now FM 2100, where it crossed present State Highway 146, continuing through what was then Main Street of Barbers Hill, now Loop 207. Today the loop curves around to reintersect State Highway 146, but back then, it made a sharp ninety-degree turn to the right to merge into present 146 and continue on to Baytown on its present route.*[212]

Adelene Stevens, another longtime resident of Dayon and daughter of Will Graves, said that her father and Chester Holbrook Sr. (see Chester and Holbrook Streets) of Holbrook & Graves Contractors laid out the present route and constructed the road between 1941 and 1946.[213] Resident Sandra Voytek grew up in Baytown but had a family farm at Devers and remembers traveling the road often in the early 1950s when it had a shell surface.[214]

In 2011, major construction to the highway took place, replacing the two lanes with four and including a turn lane down the middle from Dayton to Mont Belvieu.

Sterling Street

Sterling Street, originally called Baltic,[215] was renamed for three generations of the Sterling family. The first generation was James Bennett and Ophelia Dodd Sterling, the second generation was James "Jim" Bennett Jr. and Betty Sherman Sterling and the third was James "Jimmy" Bennett Sterling III and Benjamin "Ben" Garland Sterling.

The street was renamed between 1961 and 1963 when Jim Sterling was mayor, which was also the time when home mail delivery began in Dayton. Several streets were unnamed, so the city council formed a committee to name them. On Sterling's recommendation, eleven streets were renamed after Dayton servicemen who lost their lives during World War II. The others were named after Dayton residents or people who contributed to the development of Dayton.

James Bennett Sterling Sr. was a native of Anahuac, one of twelve children. He moved to Dayton prior to 1913 to help operate Humble Oil Company, founded by his older brother Ross (see Ross Street). He met a young lady, Ophelia Dodd, who had moved to Dayton from Orange and was the music teacher at the school. They married in 1913 and were members of the First United Methodist Church, where she was church pianist. They began their family on May 8, 1916, with the birth of their only child, James "Jim" Bennett Jr. He was born at the family's home, which was located where the Sterling Funeral Home, on the corner of Main and Kay Streets, is today.

Ophelia and James Sterling. *Courtesy of Betty Sterling*

James "Jim" Bennett Sterling Jr. graduated from Dayton High School in 1934 and was a member of the Dayton Bronco Regional Football Championship Team and of the band. He graduated from Texas A&M University in 1938, where he was a member of the Fightin' Texas Aggie Band. While at A&M, Jim worked for a funeral home opening and closing graves and also obtained his funeral home license. He felt that the funeral business was a way to help people but didn't give much thought at that point to making it a career.

After graduation, Jim returned to Dayton to assist his father in the oil and cattle business. Following the death of his father in 1941, he was appointed bulk agent for Humble Oil and Refining Company (now Exxon), a position that he held for over fifty years, assisted by his son Ben. Jim was a veteran of World War II, having served as an aerial gunner in the Army Air Corps. He married Betty Rae Sherman in January 1948.

Jim and Betty Sterling. *Courtesy of Betty Sterling*

Betty Rae Sherman was born on June 2, 1926, in Anahuac to Normie and Mary Stephenson Sherman and was the fifth of six children: a brother, Hoyle W., and sisters Esther Lou Sherman Fourcade, Neva Sherman Yount, Mary Faye Sherman and Lil Sherman Arterberry. During high school, Betty was in the band. After Pearl Harbor was attacked on December 7, 1941, she and a group of friends kept watch for enemy planes from the roof of the Anahuac Courthouse. When a plane was seen or heard, they called on their direct line to the air base at Ellington Field to report the information.

After high school graduation in 1943, Betty entered John Sealy College of Nursing (now University of Texas Medical Branch) in Galveston as a member of the newly formed Cadet Nurse Corps. She earned her registered nurse diploma in 1946 and was involved in private duty nursing in Houston, during which time she spent several days with the American Red Cross following the April 1947 Texas City disaster in which two ships exploded, killing more than five hundred and injuring thousands of people. She has since given the first endowed nursing scholarship to the UTMB School of Nursing and is serving as an honorary member of the advisory council.

In July 1947, Betty moved to Dayton, where she was employed by Dr. Ernest Rowland Richter Sr. as a nurse for the newly constructed Dayton Memorial Hospital. (Dr. Richter practiced medicine in Dayton from 1936 to 1980). After her marriage to Jim in 1948, she assisted him in his business ventures, which included his role at Humble Oil Co. and with his Brahman cattle ranch.

The Sterlings' home was bought in 1947 by Pace-Stancil Funeral Home and operated until 1962, when it was sold to Allison Funeral Home. A few months after Allison began business, Jim and Betty bought back the family home to begin Sterling Funeral Home. Betty obtained her funeral director's license in 1963 so that she could help build the family business. In 1964, while an addition was being added to the funeral home, a fire destroyed the entire place.

The present Sterling Funeral Home building was constructed soon thereafter in seventy-eight days. Jim and Betty and, later, their son Jimmy owned and operated Sterling Funeral Homes in Dayton and Anahuac for over thirty years. They also had a monument company and began the Palms Memorial Park Cemetery in Dayton, conducting community Memorial Day and Easter sunrise services for many years.

Jim was a breeder of registered Brahman cattle and registered quarter horses. He contributed many scramble calves to the Trinity Valley Exposition, for which he served as president and director. He and Betty were members of the First United Methodist Church, where Jim served on the official board and the building committee for the new sanctuary and Betty taught Sunday school and assisted with vacation Bible school. They donated the pipe organ for the new sanctuary in memory of Jim's mother, who was the first church organist.

Jim served two terms on the Dayton City Council, securing the right of way for the new four-lane highway through town, and served two terms as mayor of Dayton. He was a member of the Dayton Volunteer Fire Department serving in every position, including fire chief, and helped with the Texas City disaster in 1947. His memberships included the Sons of the American Revolution, Sons of the Republic of Texas, Sons of Confederate Veterans and the Dayton American Legion Post 512. He made many contributions to Texas A&M University and was named "Conservation Rancher of the Year" in 1983 by the Lower Trinity Valley Conservation District.

Betty's memberships have included Lakata Club, Priscilla Club, Stitch and Chatter Club, Franklin Hardin Chapter of Daughters of the Republic of Texas, the Libertad Chapter of the Daughters of the American Revolution and the Liberty County A&M Mother's Club.

Left: Jimmy Sterling. *Courtesy of Betty Sterling. Right*: Ben Sterling. *Courtesy of Betty Sterling.*

James B. Sterling Sr. passed away on December 21, 1941, and Ophelia Dodd Sterling died on August 28, 1949. Both are buried at Palms Memorial Park Cemetery. Jim Sterling passed away on March 9, 2004, following a lengthy illness and is also buried at Palms in Dayton.

Jim and Betty's two sons, James "Jimmy" Bennett III and Benjamin "Ben" Garland, were thirteen and seven when Sterling Street was named. Jimmy was born on November 4, 1949, and graduated from Dayton High School in 1967. He went to Texas A&M, where he was a member of the Fightin' Texas Aggie Band for two years. After graduating in 1971 with a degree in marine transportation, he worked on a ship for a year and then went to Baylor University to get his bachelor of business administration degree. Jim joined the family mortuary business in 1975 and worked there until 1991, when the business was sold. He married Karen Hinton from Crosby in 1973, and they had two children, Jennifer and Philip. After the family sold Sterling Funeral Home, Jim established a real estate business in Liberty called Sterling Realty. He remarried in 1995 to Sandra Kittrell, an accomplished pianist, of Liberty. The two reside there and are very active in their community.

Ben was born on July 19, 1954, and graduated from Dayton High School in 1972. He also went to Texas A&M, graduating in 1976. Ben returned to Dayton to assist his father with the Sterling Oil Company business and worked there until its sale in 1988. He became a stockbroker with the Edward Jones Company and married Linda Harding in 1993. The two lived a number of years in Clear Lake, where Ben continued in the broker business and Linda taught high school English in Baytown. The retired couple resides in Austin.[216]

Stevens Street

Stevens Street was originally named Third Avenue.[217] It is another of the eleven streets renamed by the Dayton City Council in 1961 for Dayton servicemen killed in World War II. The street is named after Calvin Ray Stevens, son of Mrs. Ida S. Lewis.

Ray Stevens. *Courtesy of the* Liberty Vindicator.

The Dayton High School yearbook for 1937–38 listed Ray Stevens as "the little fellow who played center for the Broncos." He was a two-time all-district football player and was co-captain for the 1938–39 season. Ray also played basketball in 1937 and 1938, was vice-president of his junior class and was in the junior class play entitled *Spooky Tavern*. He served on the student council and graduated in 1939.[218]

Ray entered the U.S. Navy in 1941 and was assigned as a gunners mate aboard the light cruiser USS *Boise*, commanded by Captain Mike Moran. He was killed in the Battle of Cape Esperance on October 12, 1942. As related in newspaper accounts after the battle, the *Boise*, with Stevens serving deep in number three turret as an ammunition handler, was the lead ship in a column of U.S. cruisers and destroyers that intercepted a similarly sized column of Japanese ships in the night off Cape Esperance on Guadalcanal. In twenty-seven minutes, the *Boise*'s gunners played a starring role in sinking five Japanese ships in succession, some with bigger guns than it had. The ship took tremendous fire itself, and an eight-inch shell struck below the water line at the number three turret, killing Stevens and many of the gun crew below decks.

Stevens's body was buried at sea, and he is listed on the Sea Tablets of the Missing at Manila American Cemetery in Manila, Philippines. He posthumously received the Purple Heart.[219]

A very moving memorial service was held at First Baptist Church, conducted by his pastor, Reverend Lee Hemphill. His high school English teacher, Martha Anne Turner, wrote a poem about her student:

"Somewhere at Sea"
(A Tribute to Ray Stevens of Dayton, Who Recently Was Killed in Action)

The way he looked at you,
Chin out-thrust a respectable angle,
Brown eyes, glinting mischief,
Countenance a perpetual grin,
Making perceptible a jagged front tooth—
Prize trophy collected in a high school football game.
The way he talked—
You know, crisp and staccato-like,
Rushing his words incorrigibly together sometimes
And at others drawling certain ones
Peculiarly like a lazy East Texan,
Jerking his blond, cowlicked forehead
Suddenly to one side for emphasis…

The funny way he walked—
The brisk stride of him—You see he wasn't noticeably tall,
And always he went hurrying.
And that inevitable lift of his right hand,
That invariable "Hiya, pal,"
As he passed.
The way you could count on him,
That is, depend on him,

Which is probably the way
His shipmates in the Pacific
Remembered Ray
When they left his body
His clean American body,
Somewhere at Sea.

Stone Street

Howard Stone. *Courtesy of Howard Stone.*

Stone Street is named for Howard Lonnie Stone, who came to Dayton in September 1949 to teach school. Born to Lonnie and Mary Pearl Sowell Stone on September 18, 1924, Howard grew up in Nacogdoches, Texas, graduating from Nacogdoches High School in 1942. He didn't travel far to attend college: he chose to attend Stephen F. Austin State College (now University) in Nacogdoches, where he graduated with his bachelor's degree and returned for his master's degree, graduating in 1951.

While at Stephen F. Austin State College, Howard met his future wife, Dollie Thames. After dating for two years in college, Howard and Dollie married on August 30, five days prior to starting their teaching careers in Dayton.

The Stones settled into Dayton, where Howard taught sixth grade, while Dollie taught fifth grade. The principal at the school was Miss Fredda Nottingham, and the superintendent was Lloyd Gilbert.

After teaching for two years, Howard made a life-changing decision to leave the educational field and go into banking. "Dayton ISD paid $200 per month, and the bank offered to pay $250," he said. Thus, in 1951, he began working at Dayton State Bank as a teller. He moved up the ladder until he became bank president when M.W. Ford Jr. retired. Howard stayed on as a board director until the bank sold in 1999.

That year was also a sad one for the Stones. Their beloved son, Stephen Patrick Stone, died after a seventeen-year battle with cancer. Stephen had been a lieutenant in the U.S. Navy.

Howard became very good friends with Jim Sterling and was his campaign manager when he ran for mayor in 1961. Sterling named several streets while mayor, and he named this one for his friend Howard. Stone served on the Dayton City Council for four years, beginning in 1954, and was also active in the Dayton Lions Club. In his spare time, he enjoyed golfing and visiting with friends.[220] Howard passed away on September 25, 2011, and is buried at Magnolia Park Cemetery in Dayton.

Sunset Heights

Sunset Heights was developed from land that R.C. and Genevieve Brown bought about 1940. They willed the land to their children in the early 1970s and Burney, Daryl, Don and Gene Brown developed it into the subdivision in 1972 or '73. It was so named because Gene thought it was a great location to watch the sun go down. The first house was built by Trevor Boyce.[221]

Susan Street

This street was named for Susan Friedman by her father, Saul, who developed several subdivisions in Dayton. Susan was born in Dayton in 1947 to Saul and Elaine Friedman. She had one sibling, a brother named Stephen. Her family moved to Houston in 1956 when she was nine years old. Susan graduated from Bellaire High School in 1965 and from the University of Arizona.

Susan married Dr. Allan Kaplan. She had a very impressive business career: she began working for Merrill Lynch in Houston and and then moved to New York City, where she rose to the position of Canadian bond trader. Later, she moved back to Houston and was the manager of three

Susan Friedman. *Courtesy of Saul Friedman.*

Ellis Taylor. *Courtesy of Gayle Taylor.*

well-known ladies' stores: Laurel (a division of Escada), Armani Emporium and Mondi.[222] Susan married Hiram Trimble Davis on September 24, 2011, and they reside in Austin, Texas.[223]

Taylor Lane

Taylor Lane is named for Clite Ellis and Ruth Gertrude "Gertie" Taylor. Ellis was born in 1907 in Ohio County, Kentucky, and worked in Orange, Texas, prior to moving to Dayton in 1930 with his bride, Gertie, who was a native of Orange. Ellis served in the U.S. Army during World War II

In 1945 or '46, Ellis went into business with Chester Holbrook (see Aaron, Chester and Holbrook Streets), purchasing and operating the Hudson Motor Car Dealership. But since they could purchase only four vehicles per month to sell due to war shortages, Ellis couldn't make a living, so he began an insurance company that sold policies for life, auto, casualty and property. Later, he operated the Magnolia Oil Service Station. He and Holbrook were lifelong friends and business partners, venturing into rice farming and operating the Lone Star Beer Distributing Company of Dayton. Ellis also worked at Gulf States Utilities for eighteen years.[224]

Ellis was an avid hunter of geese and ducks in area rice fields. He also loved horses and raised a half dozen or more on his land. He was known in Dayton as a gentleman.

Gertie Taylor. *Courtesy of Gayle Taylor.*

Gertie was a homemaker and a member of the Methodist Church, and she loved to go fishing. The Taylors, who had no children, frequented a place on Double Bayou in Anahuac owned by Chester Holbrook, where they and several friends would go to relax and catch fish. The Taylors owned a mobile home that they moved onto the property for all to use.[225]

The Taylors owned twenty-five acres north of and including Taylor Lane and lived on the street bearing their name. They sold five of the acres to D.E. (Doss Edward) Smith Jr. about 1963, who divided them into five lots for houses.[226] Ellis passed away on September 20, 1994, in Liberty,[227] and Gertie passed away on April 12, 1998.[228] Both are buried at Magnolia Park Cemetery in Dayton.

Timber Lane

The name of this street was chosen because land around it was very wooded. This was the first street developed in the Suburban Acres subdivision. Work began in 1964 by the children of W.T. and Allene Jamison (see Jamison Street), who formed a development partnership headed by James Robert "Bob" Jamison.[229]

Tram Road

Tram Road is the small road section remaining of a sixteen-mile railway that connected the Dayton Lumber Company, which was located on what is now Waco Street, to the Trinity Valley and Northern Railroad north of Dayton.

In 1906, when the Dayton Lumber Company (see Waco Street section) borrowed money to begin construction, it was with the stipulation that the company also build sixteen miles of standard-gauge tram road, equipped with thirty-pound iron rails. This same year, the Dayton Lumber Company proprietors chartered the Trinity Valley and Northern Railroad and laid thirty-pound rails to Rosswood, a log camp located in the "pineries" several miles north of Dayton.[230]

In 1910, the Texas and New Orleans Railroad leased eighteen miles of fifty-pound relayer rails to Dayton Lumber Company, and the owners completely rebuilt the road bed, extending it all the way to Lamb (Hightower). An article in the *American Lumberman* in 1906 recalled, "It is proposed to build a road from Dayton…to Cleveland, a distance of 25 miles. This is the tram road of the Dayton Lumber Company, recently incorporated, and which is building a mill about three miles from Dayton."

The first ten miles of the road were so straight that there was only one slight curve in it. The *Southern Industrial and Lumber Review* in January 1909 described the tram road as follows:

> *Instead of a "streak of rust," as the tram roads are so often called, it* [the Trinity Valley road] *is a ballasted road, the ballast being hauled on flat cars, and laid with 50-pound rails, every foot of the way, on hews ties, mostly of oak. The log trains run as smoothly over this road as they would over the main line of the Southern Pacific. Instead of using "dinky" engines, they use real locomotives and burn no wood for fuel, only coal. The main line engine is a 50-ton Mogul, purchased from the Southern Pacific…The heaviest locomotive stays on the main line, while the smaller ones run on the spurs, switch out the loads, and look after the steel gang.*

In the 1920s, when all of the hardwood timber was gone, the mill was sold and later torn down. The tracks on the tram road were dismantled two or three years after the mill closed. Only a small portion of the original tram road remains, now a street named Tram Road.

Tucker Street

Robert Tucker. *Courtesy of Tom Tucker.*

Tucker Street was named for Robert S. Tucker, born on February 28, 1933, in Liberty, Texas, to Rex and Alma Tucker. He grew up with siblings Rex Jr., Eli Jordan and Helen and graduated from Liberty High School in 1951. Robert, a civil attorney, received his law degree from Baylor School of Law in 1958 and set up his law practice in Liberty. That same year, he married Mary Lena Damek from Dayton, and they had one child, William Thomas "Tommy."

The Tuckers moved to Dayton in 1961 after building a new home. Robert also relocated his law practice to Dayton. His clients included Dayton State Bank as well as the W.T. Jamison family; Mr. Jamison was president of the bank. When the Jamisons developed the Suburban Acres subdivision in 1964, they named one of the streets after Tucker.

Robert was a thirty-second-degree Mason. He loved the outdoors and enjoyed bird hunting, deer hunting and saltwater fishing. His son Tom related that his dad was the most intelligent person he ever met. He was a voracious reader, sometimes reading two novels a day. He was extremely knowledgeable about a multitude of subjects, from everyday common sense matters to complex intellectual subjects.

Tom additionally said that his dad chose to practice law because he wanted to help people. He didn't die a wealthy man and retired from actively practicing law when the quest for money in his profession overtook the desire to help clients. He always championed the underdog and helped people even when they couldn't afford to pay him. Tom said that his first shotgun, a twenty gauge, and his first deer rifle, a marlin .30-30, were taken in trade from a client who didn't have money to pay for his dad's services.

Robert Tucker passed away in October 2007. He was cremated and his ashes spread at Bird Island on Matagorda Bay in accordance with his wishes.[231]

U.S. Highway 90 (Old Spanish Trail)

A 1912 picture taken in Dayton from the south facing present Main Street shows fenced pasture land with no hint of the major highway that was to come. Visionaries began to dream of a highway that would connect the southern states, making travel easier for people in their automobiles, which were rapidly replacing the horse and buggy. This dream eventually included Dayton, with the highway running through the middle of town.

The Old Spanish Trail Highway project was first conceived in 1915 to connect St. Augustine, Florida, to New Orleans. On December 11 and 12 of that year, 419 enthusiasts held a meeting in Mobile, Alabama, to promote a paved automobile highway connecting the two points, but by 1919, the vision grew to include six centers of historical interest: St. Augustine, New Orleans, San Antonio, El Paso, Tucson and San Diego, connecting the historic missions and forts built on the original Old Spanish Trail.

The original Old Spanish Trail is actually a combination of known trails established by Spanish explorers, trappers and traders used by the colonial countries of Spain, France and England in the 1600s and 1700s. Each of the eight states through which the auto route runs claims original Spanish trails that were trade routes and cattle drive trails. Many missions were constructed along these trails in the 1700s, and after the Mexican War in 1846–'47, the U.S. government established a chain of forts along them.

This 1912 picture shows Main Street from the south before Highway 90 was constructed. Visible is the Dayton Mercantile building, Cook Street, the Greer Hotel and the Masonic Lodge. *Courtesy of* Texas Illustrated Magazine.

The men planning the new Old Spanish Trail project went to their meeting with fire and determination to open this southern country, but none of them realized the financial and engineering difficulties that faced them. Funding for the project was provided by the states and counties through which the Old Spanish Trail would pass. Initial paving began in Florida and went well. Then the Great War, World War I, slowed highway design and construction funding, but annual conferences for the Old Spanish Trail continued, with Houston as the site in July 1919. There, the decision was made to ask San Antonio to lead the movement across Texas, with Harral Ayres chosen as managing director and the Gunter Hotel in San Antonio as headquarters.

In November 1919, the San Antonio conference gathered pledges for Texas, and councilors advised every Old Spanish Trail city and town to advise travelers of conditions and accommodations.

One mighty task was building the bridges to span the rivers and basins, as two-thirds of the drainage water of the United States crossed Old Spanish Trail country. The cost of this construction proved too expensive for the states, and federal help was sought. Between June and December 1922, Mr. Ayres was in Washington, D.C., gathering signatures of a majority of senators and congressmen to declare the Old Spanish Trail a basic trunk line of the U.S. highway system and ensure that every mile of it was included in federal aid mileage. J.M. Wainwright of the U.S. War Department declared the highway an essential element of U.S. defense. In August 1922, the Old Spanish Trail was placed on General John Pershing's U.S. military route map, ensuring funding for a continuous gulf and borderlands highway. Those expensive bridges and seawalls began to be funded. By 1928, $70 million had been spent. Another $40 million was needed to complete it. In April 1929, the first motorcade ran from San Diego, California, to St. Augustine, Florida. In October 1929, a return motorcade ran from St. Augustine to San Diego.[232]

Road construction through Dayton proceeded with horses hitched to graders that were used to level the ground. The Old Spanish Trail was officially designated State Highway 3 according to the Texas Department of Transportation, and the name was changed to U.S. Highway 90 between 1931 and 1940.[233] Lifelong resident Robert "Bobby" Harris said the highway was paved through Dayton in 1928 or '29.[234] The first stoplight in Dayton was installed at the intersection of Main Street and U.S. Highway 90 in 1934.[235]

Prior to this constructed highway, travel to Liberty from Dayton was on the Old Liberty Road. According to Pomella Eaton, who moved to Dayton in 1920:

By 1912, the mill owners fell on hard times, and the company was reorganized with Ross Sterling (an original stockholder) as the new president (see Ross Street). The new owners changed the name to Dayton Mills Company.

In 1920, Sterling and his partners sold the Dayton Mills Company to the South Texas Hardwood Company of Harris County. After the 1920s, the company ceased to operate, leaving many unemployed.[239]

Joseph "Joe" Denton Harris Jr., one of those unemployed, bought the small lumberyard attached to the sawmill in 1929 and operated it there for a short while before moving it to the rice warehouse, which was empty because the rice farmers were also experiencing rough times. It was located on Main Street beside the railroad tracks. He retained the original name Dayton Lumber Company

In 1936, Harris built a steam-powered sawmill on the west side of Dayton just north of the Southern Pacific Railroad and on the west side of the old Trinity Valley & Northern Railroad tracks (on present-day Waco Street). The lumberyard, now named Peoples Lumber and Feed Company because of the buying of Peoples Feed Store in 1930 and the merging of the two businesses, was moved out to the sawmill site. Oil fields had also become a principal source of business, so the name was changed again to Peoples Lumber & Supply Company. This name stuck until 1978. A concrete business was added in 1961.

After 1936 and into the 1950s, the principal part of the business was the sawmill and wholesale lumber sales. By 1955, the lack of timber and labor made further operation of the sawmill impractical. A construction operation, which had been developing since 1946, replaced the mill operation, so Pelco Construction Company was formed and the building part of the business separated from the lumberyard in 1968, both being operated by Joseph "Joe" Denton Harris III and Robert "Bobby" Dunn Harris, sons of J.D. Harris Jr.

In 1978, the lumber and material business was moved to its present location in Town Center, where it expanded and again changed its name to Peoples Building Center.[240] The concrete business was sold and remained at the Waco Street site, where it is located as of this writing.

Waring Street

Waring Street was first called Avenue F.[241] It is named for Willie B. Waring, a Dayton serviceman killed in World War II. Willie was born on October 19, 1923, to Mr. and Mrs. W.B. Waring and had two older siblings: a sister,

Willie Waring. *Courtesy of the* Liberty Vindicator.

Frances Waring Sisk, and a brother, George "Tommy." Toby Waring, a nephew, related that his father, Tommy, spoke of his brother as loving to hunt and fish as he grew up.[242]

Willie joined the U.S. Marines in 1942 before he was eighteen years old, so his parents had to sign for him to enter. He trained in California and overseas in New Zealand and fought at Bougainville and Guadalcanal before taking part in the campaign against Guam in the South Pacific. Having served for two years, Private First Class Waring was killed by enemy action on July 27, 1944, on Guam Island at the age of twenty. He is buried at Magnolia Park Cemetery in Dayton and was survived by his parents; his brother, Tommy; and his sister, Frances.[243]

Westwood Street

Westwood Street, developed in 1977, was named for Randy West. He and partner David Parker (see Park Place section) owned a total of forty-two acres that they subdivided into lots and sold. This subdivision became two streets: Westwood and Park Place.

Randy West. *Courtesy of Randy West.*

Randy was born in Farmersville, Louisiana, on January 24, 1949, to James and Doris Self West. He grew up with a sister, Cynthia West Carroll, and the family moved to Dayton in 1960. Randy graduated from Dayton High School in 1967. He enlisted in the U.S. Air Force, serving in Vietnam with the 101st Air Borne from 1970 to 1971.

After his service ended, he attended Lee College and became a carpenter by occupation. He married Sue Copeland in 1984, and they have four children: Julie and Leslie West, Joey Stinett and Angela Wells. Randy is co-owner of a construction company in La Porte. He enjoys spending time with his children and eight grandchildren. Randy is an avid hunter and fisherman, and his family shares those ventures with him.[244]

Whitewing

This is one of the streets in the Suburban Acres subdivision on which development began in 1964 by the children of W.T. and Allene Jamison (see Jamison Street). The name was chosen because it was prairie land, and whitewings were among the many birds easily seen in the area.[245]

Willow Street

This street was so named because the other streets in the subdivision were named for trees that grew in the area, and another tree name was needed. This was one of four streets developed in the Dayton Heights subdivision from twelve acres beginning in 1957 by the Trinity Development Company. Bucky Buchanan headed the company, which was also owned by Bobby Harris and Joe Harris, prominent Dayton businessmen; Bobby Roberts, vice-president of the Liberty National Bank; and possibly Marvin Henry, the surveyor for the development. The other streets laid out by the company were Cypress (now Lawrence), Oak and Pine.[246]

Winfree

Winfree is a major street running north and south through Dayton, connecting to the south with the Old River community in Chambers County. Originally named Main Street,[247] it was renamed for several members of the Winfree family, pioneers who had arrived before 1830, established a family dynasty and formed a strong network of kinship through intermarriage with other early families. Brothers Benjamin and Philip Winfree arrived about 1827 from Natchitoches Parish in Louisiana. Benjamin and his son Absalom Jesse, generally referred to as A.B.J., selected prairie land west of the Trinity River and north of Point Barrow. Benjamin received a land grant in 1831 to land west and southwest of Cotton Lake. He received the deed to this land on October 7, 1835.

A.B.J. and his brother, Jacob Freland Winfree, received headrights (4,606 acres) to land in 1835 also. Their names appear on the list of voters and landowners in an 1836 election to select a delegate to the convention that would draft the Texas Declaration of Independence. Another election gave twenty-one votes for Sam Houston as president of the Republic of Texas.

A.B.J. Winfree (circa 1803–1842) and his wife, Charlotte Millard Winfree, had seven children. The family settled on the land grant inherited from his father. Another grant in A.B.J.'s name comprises the greatest portion of present-day Cove. The area soon came to be known to early settlers as "Winfree's Cove." A.B.J. operated a ferry across Cotton Bayou. The Winfrees ran cattle and were instrumental, along with several other families, in making what is now Chambers County (which was part of Liberty County at the time; Chambers County was organized in 1858), one of the most important cattle-producing areas before the Civil War. When A.B.J. died in 1842, he left behind a considerable estate in land, cattle, property and slaves. His brother, Jacob Freland Winfree, was appointed administrator of the estate.

Jacob Freland and Mary Winfree adopted a baby whom they named Zachary Taylor Winfree, born on December 19, 1846. By the tine Chambers County was formed, the Jacob Winfree family owned twelve slaves. Zachary Taylor Winfree became a significant character in the history of West Chambers County. He married Mary Catherin Fisher (1850–1930) on March 14, 1864, and they are listed on the census of 1880 as living in the Barbers Hill area. The 1885 map of residences in the area, drawn by Grover W. Grover shows the family living on what Grover terms "Barbours Hill Settlement." A post office was established in the spring of 1890 with Zachary Taylor Winfree as the first postmaster, and it was

Zachary Taylor Winfree. *Courtesy of* Texas Illustrated Magazine.

operated out of his home. A common school district, styled Barbers Hill School Community No. 12, was organized in 1877, with Zachary Taylor Winfree as one of three trustees.[248]

Zachary Taylor Winfree was baptized in 1888 at age forty-two, and "from that moment on, Taylor Winfree dedicated his life to the service of the Maker, he himself becoming an evangelist. Traveling throughout southeast Texas preaching the Word of God, organizing new congregations and working to strengthen existing ones, most of his travels were conducted in his own one-horse buggy. The monetary rewards were small."[249]

"Generally a soft-spoken man, Zachary Taylor Winfree was known to become one of the proverbial 'hellfire and brimstone' preachers once behind the pulpit and absorbed in God's teachings."[250] Taylor Winfree is mentioned in a handwritten history of Mrs. Tom Day as preaching at the Baptist Church (see Church Street) in Dayton in 1892 when they were "between preachers."[251] He also founded a Church of Christ congregation in 1908 with eight original members. Services were held on the east bank of Cotton Bayou, but they were eventually moved to the Cove schoolhouse. A church building was later erected in the 1930s and is still standing.

The descendants of the Winfree family continued to raise cattle and assume responsible roles in the communities of Cove and Barbers Hill.

Young Street

In 1961, the Dayton City Council renamed eleven streets to honor Dayton's servicemen killed in World War II, this being one of them. Originally called Fourth Avenue,[252] it is named for Charles Stenius "Bubba" Young, born on April 10, 1920, the son of Mr. and Mrs. R.V. Young, whose family lived on this street. While at Dayton High School, Young played tuba in the band and graduated in 1938. He attended Southwestern Louisiana Institute (now the University of Louisiana) at Lafayette, Louisiana, and Texas University (University of Texas), where he studied medicine.

Young enlisted with the Royal Canadian Air Force in October 1941 and received his wings on September 10, 1942, being awarded a Silver Plaque as an award of merit given to the 8 outstanding men in the class of 1,280. He was then stationed in Great Britain with the Royal Air Force's Fourth Eagle Squadron and made twenty-five missions for England, earning a decoration for wounds received in combat.

Bubba Young. *Courtesy of the* Liberty Vindicator.

Lieutenant Young was commissioned a flight officer with the U.S. Army Air Corps on March 24, 1943. He piloted a Mosquito medium bomber known as "Liberty Lass" and once dined with King George and Queen Elizabeth of England.

In July 1943, Young was sent to the Mediterranean to support landings in Sicily and participated in the famed air raid on the Ploesti oil fields in Romania, helping knock out one-third of Germany's oil supplies. His was the only surviving plane of a squadron of nine on that raid. He acted as gunner when the waist gunner was killed before the target was reached, after which he was returned to a rest home in England for treatment of combat fatigue. Young received the Distinguished Flying Cross for bravery on this mission, one of thirty he flew in the Mediterranean Sea area.

After he recovered, he was transferred for training in P-38 fighter planes. He was killed in a training accident on June 6, 1944. In his career, he earned two Distinguished Flying Crosses, the Air Medal with four Oak Leaf Clusters, a special citation for completing twenty-five missions and the British Decoration for Wounds. He was one of the most decorated men from Liberty County to fly in the skies against Germany. He was survived by his parents and two sisters.[253]

Young is buried at Fort Sam Houston National Cemetery in San Antonio.

Zylks Road

This short road is located on land owned by Melvin "Pete" Giles Zylks, who moved to Dayton in 1973 to begin farming. He was born on July 23, 1932, at Rodessa, Louisiana, to Samuel Gensel Sr. and Viola Shaw Zylks. He was the second-youngest of nine children.

Growing up in Rodessa, Pete played high school football and graduated from Rodessa High School in 1950. His future wife, Bobbie Alford, was a

Pete Zylks. *Courtesy Bobbie Zylks.*

cheerleader there and graduated in 1951. They were high school sweethearts, marrying on June 7, 1952.

After high school graduation, Pete was a pipeline welder for a few years, and later, he and Bobbie owned and operated a dairy in Hooks, Texas, close to Texarkana for many years.

Pete's good friend Thomas Laurie Drawhorn farmed rice in Dayton and encouraged him to buy into his farm and move here. Pete arrived the year before, bringing his family in 1974 because his son needed to graduate from high school back in Hooks. Pete and Bobbie raised three children: Kathy Zylks Majors, Melvin Giles Zylks Jr. and Pattie Zylkes Bales, who graduated from Dayton High School.

Pete loved farming, cultivating rice and soybeans for several years before independent farming was no longer profitable, forcing him to retire. He remained very active, pursuing his love of horses by exercising and riding them for Myron McDowell and for a barn in Crosby. Pete remained an avid football fan and enjoyed playing golf. An illness claimed his life in 2008, and he is buried at Rodessa, Louisiana.[254]

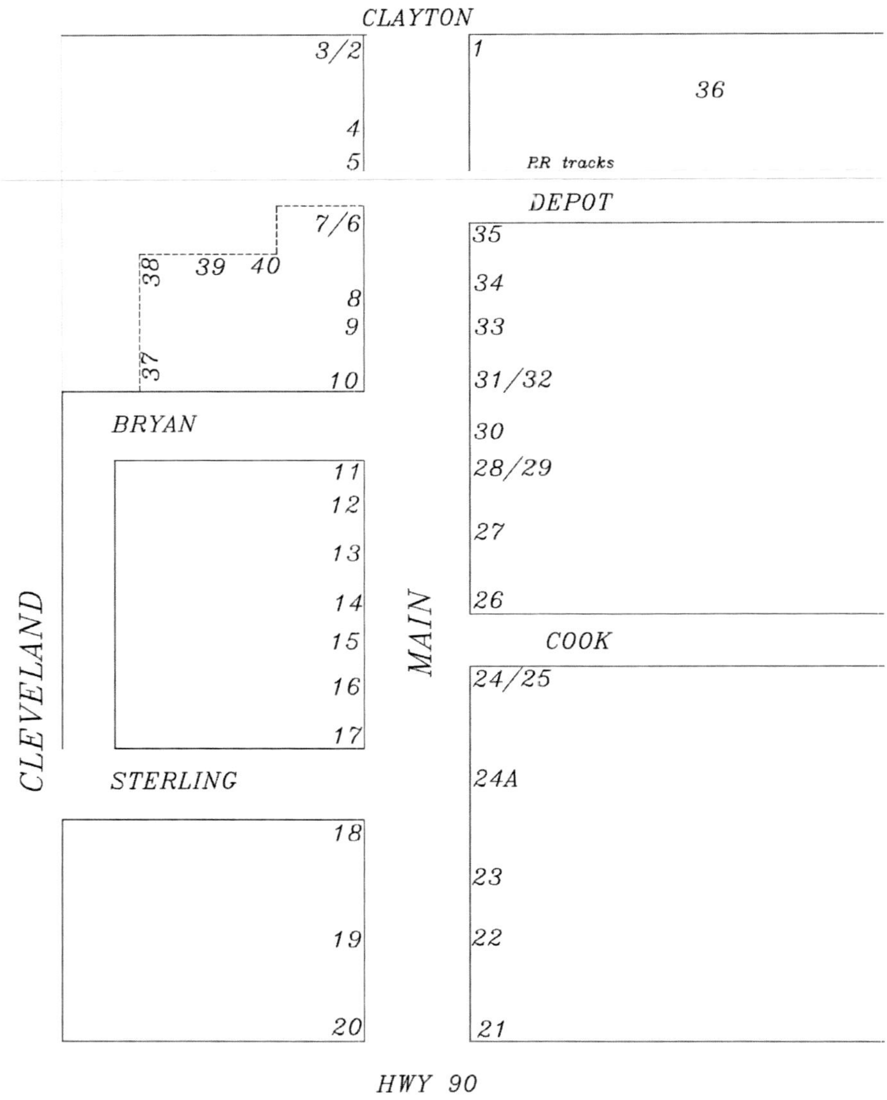

Business locations on historic Main Street. *Courtesy of Liberty County Central Appraisal District.*

HISTORIC MAIN STREET BUSINESSES

The following list of businesses on Main is not exhaustive but notes many businesses at various times in Dayton's history.

1) Phillips Gas Station / Dewey's General Store (a two-story building that included groceries)
2) Remke's Hardware and Grocery / Wilford Moreau's Feed Store
3) (behind #2) a bakery operated by a man named Colbert
4) People's Feed Store, owned by the Harris family (had a grocery store downstairs and offices upstairs) / Salon Central (different building, same location)
5) American Rice Growers office
6) Sterling Realty Company (early 1920s) / Deweese Grocery Store / Sonnier's Grocery / AP Grocery / Sav-Way Grocery (first location)
7) (second story above Sonnier's Grocery) Hotel / Dr. Ernest Richter's office (first location) and Jim and Lee Barton and Dr. Speer's dentist offices
8) Red & White Grocery Store owned by Wright
9) Heal's Pharmacy / McGinty's Pharmacy (first location)
10) U.S. Post Office (first location) / Davis' OK Cleaners / a shoe store
10A) (located behind #10) Law West of Trinity, JP Chick Hatch
11) Dayton Mercantile Bank / Richardson's Grocery / Leo Moreau's Barber Shop / Cotton's Barber Shop
12) Jansen's Grocery Store
13) Western Auto (first location)

14) Setek's Bakery
15) Jackson's Café
16) Rio Theater (built by O.B. Sterling Sr.; owned later by Ted Miller / Fowler Moore / Carol Bagley)
17) Bell Law Office / Sander's Grocery Store (second location)
17A) (located behind #17) Domino Hall
18) Hoover's Put Put Golf Course / Dayton State Bank Drive-Through / building demolished 2010 / New building: THS Medical Clinic
19) Little Folk's Café (owned by Richard and Anna Holbrook)
20) (Moore's / Crumpler's / Davis's / Oglesbee's) Humble Filling Station / Dayton State Bank (third location) / Prosperity Bank
21) Neuman's Sinclair Garage & DeSoto dealership / Hungry Hound Hamburgers / Thrifty Pharmacy / Dayton Exchange convenience store with gas pumps
22) Sanders' Grocery Store (first location) / Bob Martin's Insurance / Southern Gypsies Gifts
23) Dr. Wilson's office / Berkeley Eye Center
24) Dayton State Bank (second location) / Whitman's Cleaners / Liberty County Title and Abstract (W.A. Conner and J.E. Berry) / Conner Realty / Wes Hinch Law Office
24A) Kenneth Strahan Law Office / ATEX Realty
25) (backside of #24) Dr. Tadlock / Dayton Industrial Foundation / Edward Jones Investments
26) Jackson's Department Store (in #26 & 27) / Nelson's Jewelry / B&B Auto / **building burned March 7, 1984 / parking lot
27) Jackson's Department Store (in #26 & 27) / Sherri's Video / Sterling Professional Building / Calvary Medical Clinic
28) feed store / Ben Franklin's Variety Store / Voygt's Variety Store
29) (second story of #28) George Beauty Shop
30) Ward's Cleaners / LaCour's Barber Shop / Daley's Barber Shop
31) Guthrie's Café / Jean Haynes' Book Store
32) (second story of #31) Dayton Hotel
33) Mansfield's Pharmacy / Quick's Pharmacy / Texas Kountry Kitchen (in #33 & 34)
34) Charlie Brumaghim's Electrical Shop / Texas Kountry Kitchen (in # 33 & 34)
35) Kline's Grocery, Clothing & Dry Goods / Jeep Bell's Dry Goods / building demolished in 2007
36) Sav Way Grocery Store (second location) / Saul's Auction House

The block of buildings on the west side of Main between the railroad tracks and Bryan Street was demolished in 2007. They represent #7–11. In their place, Day Tex Plaza was built in 2008 with the following stores:

37) Tanliners
38) Hometown Fitness
39) Elegance Hair Studio
40) Cowboy Cleaners

NOTES

Aaron Street

1. Jan Guerico, "*Vindicator*'s Rice Edition," *Liberty Vindicator*, August 18, 1982.
2. *Liberty Vindicator*, obituary for Chester Holbrook, February 25, 1990.
3. Ibid., obituary for Ellen Holbrook, February 15, 1987.

Atascocita

4. Ted Boyer, interview, February 16, 2012.

Barrow Street

5. Dayton, Liberty County, Texas Map (New York: Sanborn Map Company, 1943).
6. *Liberty Vindicator*, obituary for Douglas Barrow, April 19, 1945.

Beauty Street

7. Bobby and Carl Sanders, interview, October 2012.
8. Alphene Richter, interview, October 2012.

Benton Street

9. Pat Landwehr, e-mail received August 15, 2012.
10. *Liberty Vindicator*, obituary for A.T. Benton, August 12, 1981.

Brooks Street

11. Joann Paul, interview, March 16, 2012.

Brown Road

12. Dale Brown, interview, September 8, 2011; Norman Brown, interview, February 1, 2012.

Brown Trail

13. Patsie Arnold, Alan Dee Conner and Larry Harris, interviews, August 2011.

Bryan Street

14. Dayton, Liberty County map, 1927.
15. Ibid., 1943.
16. Betty Sterling Williamson, interview, fall 2012.

Cherry Creek Road

17. Homer Cherry, personal papers about John Cherry, Sam Houston Regional Library, Liberty, Texas.
18. Ibid.

CHESTER STREET

19. *Liberty Vindicator*, "74-Acre Plan Has Approval from Council," August 9, 1962.
20. Guerico, "*Vindicator*'s Rice Edition."
21. *Liberty Vindicator*, obituary for Chester Holbrook, February 25, 1990.
22. Ibid., obituary for Ellen Holbrook, February 15, 1987.

CHURCH STREET

23. Dayton, Liberty County map, 1927.
24. Eileen Jarrett Stoesser, *Bearing Fruit for Jesus: A History of the First Baptist Church, Dayton, Texas, 1978–1988* (self-published, 1988), 1.
25. Mrs. Frances Sansom, interview with Eileen Stoesser, August 16, 1987.
26. James Benjamin Sterling Jr., interview with Eileen Stoesser, August 29, 1988.
27. Southeast Texas Baptist Association Minutes.
28. Jack Unkel, interview with Eileen Stoesser, August 20, 1987.
29. Mrs. Helen White, interview with Eileen Stoesser, August 22, 1987.
30. Stoesser, *Bearing Fruit for Jesus*, 30.
31. Dovie Norcross, *First United Methodist Church, Dayton, Texas, 1864–1989* (self-published, 1989), unit 1, p. 2.
32. Ibid., unit 1, p. 3.
33. Ibid., unit 4, p. 1.
34. Ibid., unit 5, unpublished.

CLARENCE STREET

35. Lena Ruth Dearbonne Allen, e-mail received on June 14, 2012.

CLAYTON STREET

36. Dayton, Liberty County map, 1927.
37. Ibid., 1943.
38. *Dayton News*, "Clayton Moreau Has Anniversary Dinner," February 1942.
39. Punky Moreau Shanks, niece of Clayton Moreau, interview, March 17, 2012.

Cleveland Street and State Highway 321

40. Alphene Richter, interview, September 14, 2011.
41. Linda Blackburn Harris, interview, November 12, 2012.
42. Jack Unkel, interview, June 13, 2011.
43. Lloyd Pierce, highway engineer with TxDOT, Liberty County office, e-mail received, November 12, 2012.

Colbert Street

44. Dayton, Liberty County map, 1943.
45. W.T. Block, *East Texas Mill Towns & Ghost Towns*, vol. 2 (Lufkin, TX: Best of East Texas Publishers, 1995), 157.
46. Diane Paul, phone interview, October 9, 2011.
47. Plaque at the Rosenwald School, Dayton, Texas.

Coleman Street

48. Dayton, Liberty County map, 1927.
49. Rose Klimitchek, interview, September 9, 2011.
50. *Liberty Vindicator*, obituary for Mrs. O.H. Coleman, December 6, 1956.
51. Ibid., obituary for Oscar Coleman, April 27, 1959.

Collins Street

52. Iris Collins Eaton, phone interview, March 19, 2012.
53. John Collins, phone interview, March 20, 2012.

Daisy Street

54. Lillie Flowers, interview, August 1, 2011.

DALE STREET

55. Norman Dale Brown Jr., interview, August 9, 2011.

DEPOT STREET

56. Dayton, Liberty County map, 1927.
57. Ibid., 1943.
58. *Handbook of Texas*, vol. 6. (Austin: Texas Historical Society, 1996), 373.
59. Pomella Eaton, written recollections of Dayton, May 5, 1987.
60. *Texas Illustrated Magazine*, "Fire on Depot," May 2002.

EDGAR STREET

61. Ancestry.com.
62. *Southern Industrial and Lumber Review*, January 1909, 35–6.
63. Block, *Mill Towns & Ghost Towns*, 155.
64. Shirley Haidusek, comp., *Linney Creek Dayton, Texas* (information compiled for submission for historical marker), n.d., 2.

ELAINE STREET

65. Saul Friedman, phone interview, August 2, 2011.

EMMA STREET

66. Robert "Bobby" Harris, interview, April 25, 2011.
67. Guy Lawrence "Larry" Harris, interview, October 13, 2013.

ENTZMINGER STREET

68. Dorothea Baldwin, phone interview, June 4, 2012.
69. Mary Ann Matthews, phone interview, June 8, 2012.

ESTHER STREET

70. Saul Friedman, phone interview, August 2, 2011.

EVELYN STREET

71. Aaron James Holbrook, interview, March 2012.
72. Mary Ellen Holbrook Conner, interview, May 2012.

FLOWERS STREET

73. Dayton, Liberty County map, 1943.
74. Bill Flowers, phone interview, February 4, 2012.
75. Linda Jamison, e-mail, February 1, 2012.
76. Ibid.

FM HIGHWAY 1960

77. Lester Ray and Betty Jo Wisegerber, interview, July 30, 2013.
78. Donna Caroathers, TxDot, Liberty County office, phone interview, August 1, 2013.

FORD AVENUE

79. M.W. Ford Jr., interview, August 14, 2011.

FORDLAND ESTATES

80. John and Jessica (Ford) Johnson, interview, July 21, 2012.

FRIERY STREET

81. *Liberty Vindicator*, "Pfc. J.C. Friery Killed in Action in Pacific Area," November 2, 1944.
82. Ibid., "Killed in Action," November 9, 1944.

GLASS STREET

83. U.S. Census, Ancestry.com.
84. Wilburt Wycliff, phone interview, August 9, 2012.
85. U.S. Census, Ancestry.com.
86. Emily Wycliff, phone interview, August 9, 2012.

GOOSECREEK STREET

87. *History of Baytown* (City of Baytown: Baytown.org).
88. Block, *Mill Towns & Ghost Towns*, 148.

HARMON STREET

89. Dayton, Liberty County map, 1943.
90. E.B. Neuman, interview, September 8, 2013.
91. Martha Sell, employee of American Battle Monuments Commission, letter, August 18, 2013.
92. *Liberty Vindicator*, "Dayton Corporal Drowns on Duty," May 17, 1945.

HILL STREET

93. Dayton, Liberty County map, 1943.
94. Liberty County Central Appraisal District records.
95. Ancestry.com.

Hillcrest

96. Sandra Carraway, interview, August 25, 2011.

Holbrook Street

97. Guerico, "*Vindicator*'s Rice Edition."
98. Mary Ellen Holbrook Conner, interview, November 13, 2011.
99. *Liberty Vindicator,* obituary for Ellen Holbrook, February 15, 1987.
100. Ibid., obituary for Chester Holbrook, February 25, 1990.

Holitzke Street

101. *Liberty Vindicator,* "Flying Sergeant From Dayton Is Killed in Action," August 3, 1944.
102. Ibid., "Don Receives Daddy's Medal," March 1, 1945.
103. Joseph L. Holitzke, American Battle Monuments Commission webpage.

Holmes Street

104. M.W. Ford, interview with Kevin Ladd, September 2006.
105. Ancestry.com.

Houston Street

106. Dayton, Liberty County map, 1943.
107. Kevin Ladd and M.W. Ford, "A History and Guide to Dayton Street Names," *Texas Illustrated Magazine,* September 4, 2006.
108. Lester Ray Wisegerber, interview, July 30, 2013.
109. Betty Jo George Wisegerber, interview, July 30, 2013.

Hunnicutt Street

110. Ancestry.com.
111. Joann Paul, interview, February 2012.
112. Bobby Harris, interview, February 2012.

Jamison Street

113. Linda Jamison, phone interview, February 2012.

Juanita Street

114. Aaron James Holbrook, interview, March 2012.

Kay Street

115. Dayton, Liberty County map, 1927.
116. Ibid., 1943.
117. Edith Grantham, phone interview, November 4, 2011.
118. Punky Moreau, interview, November 2, 2011.
119. *Liberty Vindicator,* "Pfc. C.D. Kay Killed in Action on Isle of Saipan," July 20, 1944.
120. Mrs. Leo Moreau, "In Memory of Fighting Marine," 1944, copy received from Punky Moreau, November 2011.

Kerr Street

121. Ancestry.com.
122. Block, *Mill Towns & Ghost Towns*, 155.
123. *Liberty Vindicator,* "A.E. Kerr, Former Dayton Railroad and Sawmill Man, Dies," January 12, 1967.

Kindt Street

124. Mary Beth Jamison, interview, November, 2011.
125. U.S. Census records; Ancestry.com.
126. Liberty County Courthouse, *Index to Deeds, vol. E–L, 1875–April 1927*, 78.
127. *Lawton Constitution*, "Kindt Will to Be Broken," November 18, 1916.
128. Ibid., "Church Wins Case in Supreme Court Kindt Will Is Upheld," February 8, 1921.
129. Liberty County Courthouse, *Index to Deeds vol. A–L, 1875–1927*, 438.
130. Ibid., *Map Record 1 Book.*

Klemp Road

131. Alan Dee Conner, interview, June 2012.
132. *(Liberty, TX) Illustrated Press*, May 1969.

LaBlanc Lane

133. Mary LeBlanc, interview, August 12, 2013.
134. Sue Moore, interview, August 12, 2013.

LaCour Street

135. Annie Wingo, phone interview, September 11, 2012.
136. Hurley Provost, interview, October 18, 2012; Henry Dugat, phone interview, October 23, 2012.

Ladd Street

137. Block, *Mill Towns & Ghost Towns*, 150, 155.
138. www.pinebluff.com/murals.htm.
139. Ancestry.com.

LAIRD STREET

140. Curtis Laird, phone interview, March 2012.

LAWRENCE STREET

141. Ancestry.com.
142. Ibid.
143. Teresa Lawrence, interview, June 18, 2012.

LIGONS STREET

144. Joann Paul, interview, May 23, 2012.
145. Burley Gant, interview, June 8, 2012.

LINNEY STREET

146. Sam Houston Regional Library, Liberty, Texas. *Minutes of the Board of Trustees for the Town of Liberty*, vol. 1, 207.
147. Shirely Haidusek, "History of Linney Cemetery, Dayton, Texas," Linney Cemetery Association, n.d., (a copy is at Dayton's Old School Museum, Dayton, Texas).

LISA LANE

148. Lisa Wilson Gibson, interview, August 2, 2011.

LITTLE JOHN

149. Bobby Harris, interview, August 9, 2011.

LOVERS LANE

150. Chris Heinrich, phone interview, July 13, 2012.

LOWE STREET

151. Lynne Lowe Harding, interview, 2012.

LUKE STREET

152. Lois Pruitt, interview, May 2012.

MAIN STREET

153. Dayton, Liberty County map, 1927.
154. Liberty Vindicator, February 17, 1911. The author did an extensive search for a document with the 1911 date for the incorporation of Dayton at Dayton City Hall, the Sam Houston Regional Library, the Old School Museum, the Liberty County Courthouse and online. Nothing was found. The only thing found alluding to the 1911 date was the short statement in the *Vindicator. The Handbook of Texas* gives 1911 as Dayton's incorporation, but no documentation is cited.
155. Dayton City Hall. Minutes of the Dayton City Council, Dayton, Texas, 1926.
156. Ibid.

MANOR STREET

157. Lisa Wilson Gibson, interview, August 2, 2011.

MARBLEHEAD STREET

158. Mutt Neuman, interview, March 7, 2012.

McBride Street

159. Lois Pruitt, interview, October 2011.
160. Beatrice Payne, interview, January 2012.
161. Joann Paul, interview, June 2011.

Meadows Lane

162. Boyd and Patsie Arnold, interviews, December 2012.

Meremar Lane

163. Sandra Voytek, interview, February 28, 2012.

Merritt Street

164. Dayton, Liberty County map, 1943.
165. *Liberty Vindicator*, obituary of Corporal W.H. Merritt III, July 27, 1944.
166. Bill O'Neil, phone interview, February 2012.

Milo Street

167. M.W. Ford Jr., interview, August 14, 2011.

Moller Street

168. *Liberty Vindicator*, obituary of Charles Milton Moller, July 29, 1943.
169. Ancestry.com.
170. Ancestry.com.
171. Dayton City Hall. *Dayton City Council Minutes*, November 28, 1925, 4.
172. Ibid, November 28, 1928, .56.
173. *Liberty Vindicator*, obituary for C.M. Moller, July 29, 1943.
174. Norcross, *First United Methodist Church*, 6.

Myra Lane

175. Ted Boyer, private interview, February 16, 2012.

Nancy Street

176. Margie and Bernice Green, interviews, November 1, 2012.

Nelton Street

177. Dayton, Liberty County map, 1943.
178. Geneology of Amos Franklin Norcross, provided by Nell Whittington, October 29, 2012.
179. Nell Whittington, written recollections, November 16, 2012
180. Zoe Norcross, written recollections, October 9, 2012.

Norcross Lane

181. Ancestry.com, 1900 U.S. Census.
182. Ibid., 1910 U.S. Census.
183. Ancestry.com.
184. Ibid., 1920 U.S. Census.
185. Nell Whittington, written recollections, November 3, 2012.

Oak Street

186. Bobby and Larry Harris, interview, March 14, 2012.

Park Place

187. David Parker, interview, October 29, 2012.

Paul Street

188. Joann Paul, interview, February 2012.

Pine Place

189. David Parker, interview, October 29, 2012.

Prater Street

190. Sherial Lawson, phone interview, August 2013.
191. Ancestry.com, U.S. Censuses of 1870–1930.
192. Annette Lockett, phone interview, September 2012.

Pruitt Street

193. Frank W. Johnson, *A History of Texas and Texans,* vol. 5 (Chicago: American Historical Society, 1914), 2658.
194. Sam Houston Regional Library. Cemetery Records, the French Cemetery, Dayton, Texas.

River Oaks

195. Mary Beth Jamison, interview, August 25, 2011.

Ross Street

196. "Sterling, Ross Shaw," Texas State Historical Association *Handbook of Texas* online, http://www.tshaonline.org/handbook/online/articles/fst42.

Sawmill Road

197. Bobby Harris, private interview, August 13, 2012.

Seaberg Industrial Road

198. Susan Seaberg, interview, February 5, 2013.

Seekamp Street

199. Dayton, Liberty County map, 1943.
200. Candace (Seekamp) Colby, phone interview, May 16, 2012.
201. *Liberty Vindicator*, "Dayton Woman's Husband Killed in Plane Crash," August 30, 1945.

Shanks Street

202. Lester Ray Wisegerber, interview, January 28, 2012.
203. Kathryn Shanks Martin, interview, March 20, 2012.

Sherwood Drive

204. Bobby Harris, interview, June 13, 2011.

Skylark

205. Mary Beth Jamison, interview, August 25, 2011.

Slover Driver

206. Ted Boyer, interview, February 16, 2012.

Smith Street

207. Jimmy Sterling, phone interview, March 18, 2012.
208. Ancestry.com.
209. Annie Wingo, interview, February 2, 2012.

210. Betty Sterling, interview, October 8, 2012.
211. Ruth Hensarling, interview, October 14, 2012.

STATE HIGHWAY 146

212. E.B. Neuman II, interview, October 6, 2012.
213. Adelene Stevens, interview, September 13, 2012.
214. Sandra Voytek, interview, November 5, 2012.

STERLING STREET

215. Dayton, Liberty County map, 1927.
216. Betty Sterling, interview, August 2, 2012.

STEVENS STREET

217. Dayton, Liberty County map, 1943.
218. *Dayton High School Yearbook*, 1937–38.
219. *Liberty Vindicator*, "C.R. Stevens," October 1942.

STONE STREET

220. Howard Lonnie Stone, interview, August 4, 2011.

SUNSET HEIGHTS

221. Gene and Don Brown, phone interviews, July 21, 2011.

SUSAN STREET

222. Saul Friedman, phone interview, August 2011.
223. *Houston Chronicle*, "Susan Ann Friedman Weds Mr. Hiram Trimble Davis," September 25, 2011.

Taylor Lane

224. Gayle Taylor, phone interview, March 22, 2012.
225. Mary Strickland Fregia, interview, November 5, 2011.
226. Doss "Sonny" Smith, interview, March 19, 2012.
227. *Liberty Vindicator*, "Ellis Taylor," September 25, 1994.
228. Ibid., "Ruth G. 'Gertie' Taylor," April 19, 1998.

Timber Lane

229. Mary Beth Jamison, interview, August 25, 2011.

Tram Road

230. Block, *Mill Towns & Ghost Towns*, 150.

Tucker Street

231. Tom Tucker, phone interview, March 2012.

U.S. Highway 90 (Old Spanish Trail)

232. Alice Luckhardt, "Old Spanish Trail Project," http://voices.yahoo.com/old-spanish-trail-6435690.html (July 30, 2010).
233. Lloyd Pearce (TxDOT), phone interview, April 2012.
234. Bobby Harris, interview, February 2012.
235. Dayton City Hall, *Minutes of the Dayton City Council*, June 7, 1934.
236. Pomella Eaton, written recollections of Dayton, May 5, 1987.
237. Charlotte Kahl, "Old Spanish Trail Basic History," oldspanishtrailcentennial.com, 2004.

Waco Street

238. Bernice Green, interview, August 2012.
239. Block, *Mill Towns & Ghost Towns*, 150–55.
240. Robert "Bobby" D. Harris, notes written about the family business, n.d.

Waring Street

241. Dayton, Liberty County map, 1943.
242. Toby Waring, phone interview, May 15, 2011.
243. *Liberty Vindicator*, "Dayton Marine Killed by Enemy on Guam Island," August 24, 1944.

Westwood Street

244. Randy West, interview, October 22, 2012.

Whitewing

245. Mary Beth Jamison, interview, August 25, 2011.

Willow Street

246. Bobby and Larry Harris, interview, March 14, 2012.

Winfree

247. Dayton, Liberty County map, 1927.
248. Margaret Henson and Kevin Ladd, *Chambers County: A Pictorial History* (Norfolk, VA: Doning Company, 1988).
249. *The Man of Sin, The Woman in Scarlet and The Woman in White*, (1907). Noted in Stoesser, *Bearing Fruit for Jesus*, 79.

250. Kendon L. Clark, "A Diamond in the Rough," in *A History of Cove, Texas, Vol. 2, 1900–1941* (Ozark, MO: Yates Publishing Company, 1987). Noted in Stoesser, *Bearing Fruit for Jesus*, 80.
251. Stoesser, *Bearing Fruit for Jesus*, 79.

YOUNG STREET

252. Dayton, Liberty County map, 1943.
253. *Liberty Vindicator*, "Many Honors to Flier of Dayton Killed on D-Day," June 29, 1944.

ZYLKS ROAD

254. Bobbie Zylks, interview, August 24, 2011.

INDEX

A

Acie Cemetery 79, 90, 95, 96, 103, 109, 111, 123
Addington family 116
advisory board of directors (Dayton State Bank) 100
Aerial Gunnery Medal 118
agriculture teacher 94
Air Medal 17, 67, 118, 148
airplane crash 118
Akron 69
Alabama and Coushatta Indians 26
Alamo 26
Alden 36
aldermen 91, 101
Alfred Bennett Lumber Company 48, 142
Allen, Lena Ruth Dearbonne 36
Allison Funeral Home 127
Aloe Army Air Field 118
Alto, Texas 70
Ambler Street 23
American Legion 127
American Lumberman 135
American Maid Flour Mills 114
American Metals 77
American Rice Growers Association 36, 123
American Rice Growers Association board of directors 116
American Rice Growers Co-op Association of Dayton board 116
Ames Catholic Cemetery 21
Ames, Texas 21
Anahuac Courthouse 126
Anahuac, Texas 16, 35, 113, 121, 125, 126, 127, 134
Angelina River 86
Angleton 70
Angleton Business College 71
Archer City 116
Arkansas Good Roads Association 81
Army Air Corps 126
Arnold, Boyd 23, 95

Arnold Construction Company, Inc. 95
Arnold, Patsie 96
art 100
Atascocito District 25
attorney 38, 77, 119
Austin 28, 102, 121, 129, 133
Austin County 106
automobile accident 122
Avenue A 117
Avenue B 73
Avenue C 56
Avenue D 98
Avenue F 143
Ayish Bayou District 86
Ayres, Harral 138

B

Baltic 125
banker 71
banking 131
bank president 132
Baptist Church 27, 147
Barbers Hill 16, 121, 123, 146
Barbers Hill School 147
Barrow, Douglas 17
Barrow family 17
Battle of Cape Esperance 129
Battle of San Jacinto 26, 118
Battle of Tarawa 74
Battle of the Alamo 118
Baylor University 108, 128
Baytown 61, 75, 77, 114, 115, 124, 129
Baytown, Texas 39
Beach City 69
Beaumont Enterprise 142
Beaumont, Texas 98, 100
Bedias, Texas 83
Bee County 83
Bellaire High School 132
Bell County 64
Belton 103
Bennett, Alfred 142
Benton, Angus Thomas Walter 20
Benton, Eliza McLeod 18
Benton family 18, 94
Benton, Thomas J. 18
Benton, Wessie Aldridge Goodrum 20
Berry, C.F. 91, 101
Berry, J.E. 55
Best family 111
Best, James 111
Bigelow, N.P. 142
blacksmith 83, 84
Blonstein, Dr. David 54
Blonstein, Esther Friedman 53, 94
Blue Ribbon Rice Mill Board 116
board director 132
board of commissioners 112
bond election 88
Boone, Daniel 58
Bougainville 144
Boyer, Ted 17, 102, 121, 155, 168, 170
Brazoria County 70, 84
Brazos River 26
Brazos, Texas 101
Breeden, Katy 100
Brenham, Texas 85
Bridges, Matilda C. 25, 26
Bronze Star 74
Brooks, Clarence 20
Brooks family 21
Brooks, Louise Broussard 20
Brown family 22, 132
Brown, Genevieve 132
Brown, Harry 21, 23
Brown, Kimmie 21, 23
Brown, Norman 23
Brown, R.C. 132

Buchanan, Bucky 107, 145
bulk agent 126
bull riding 94
buried at sea 130
Burleson, Texas 106

C

Cadet Nurse Corps 126
Calloway, Reverend James 33
Cambridge American Cemetery 68
Cameron, B.F. 33
Camp Hood, Texas 60
Camp Shelby, Mississippi 61
Camp Springs Army Air Base, Washington, D.C. 118
Canadian bond trader 132
Candor 117
Canion, Kenneth, Sr. 38
carpenter 84, 85, 144
Catholic Church 73
Cato 73
cattle business 126
cattle drive trails 137
cattleman 116, 119
Central Appraisal District 65
Central High School 66
certified public accountant 97
Chachere, L.J. 94
Chambers County 24, 68, 69, 106, 145
Cherokee Indians 26
Cherokee War 26
Cherry family 25
Cherry, Homer 25
Cherry, John 25
China, Texas 104, 106
Christian Science Church 76
Church of Christ 147
Church Street 84, 91, 115
CIA College 53
circuit riders 29, 71
Citizens State Bank 75
Civil War 27, 146
Clayton Street 38, 105
Clear Lake 129
Cleveland Highway (State Highway 321) 37
Cleveland Street 33, 37, 89, 119
Cleveland, Texas 26, 39, 55, 135
Colbert, Annie 90
Colbert School 79, 122
Colbert Street 36, 61, 94, 95, 96
College of Industrial Arts & Sciences 53
Committee on Sanitation 101
Committee on Streets 101
community center 88
Conner, Alan Dee 23
Conner, Leard 77
Conner, Mary Ellen Holbrook 67
Conner, W.A. 77
Conroe 97
Conservation Rancher of the Year 127
construction business 121
contractors 28
cook 111
Cook Street 29, 84
Cotton Lake 146
Coushatta Indians 25
Cove 146
Cranfill-Reynolds Drilling Company 82
Creoles 109
Crosby 149
Cross Avenue 103
Curry, Bull (wrestler) 36
Curtis Publishing Company 117
Cypress Street 82

D

dairyman 101
Daisetta 89
Daniel, Susan 108
DAR Award 96, 97
Darden, Fowler, and Creighton, LLP 97
Davis, Hiram Trimble 133
Day, I.C. 142
Daystown 142
Dayton Baptist Church of Christ 29, 30
Dayton Bronco Regional Football Championship Team 125
Dayton Broncos 17, 55, 69, 73, 129
Dayton City Council 17, 18, 21, 23, 29, 38, 39, 56, 60, 72, 73, 79, 93, 100, 103, 117, 127, 129, 132, 166, 167, 172
Dayton Future Farmers of America (FFA) 87, 93
Dayton–Goose Creek Railroad 61, 62, 75, 114, 123
Dayton Heights subdivision 82, 107, 145
Dayton High School 17, 53, 54, 56, 60, 63, 67, 72, 73, 88, 95, 96, 97, 99, 108, 115, 119, 120, 125, 128, 129, 144, 147, 149, 171
Dayton High School band 125
Dayton Hill 90
Dayton Historical Society 108, 119
Dayton Independent School District (ISD) 38, 39, 131
Dayton Industrial Foundation 76
Dayton ISD board of trustees 116
Dayton ISD Educational Support Center 38, 69
Dayton ISD school board 49
Dayton Lions Club 132
Dayton Lumber Company 48, 62, 79, 80, 113, 135, 142, 143
Dayton Memorial Hospital 127
Dayton Mercantile Building 91
Dayton Mills Company 49, 75, 79, 143
Dayton Mission 32
Dayton News 36
Dayton Police Department 120
Dayton School 37
Dayton servicemen killed in World War II 17, 23, 56, 60, 63, 67, 73, 98, 117, 125, 129, 143, 147
Dayton State Bank 24, 93, 99, 113, 132, 136
Dayton State Bank board 116
Dayton Tigers 36
Dayton Volunteer Fire Department 127
Dazzler 97
deacon 85
Dearbonne, Alice Baldwin 35
Dearbonne, Clarence, Sr. 35
Dearbonne family 35
Declaration of Texas Independence 26
Democratic Party 114
Denton 53
Depew Street 64
Devers 57, 124
Dewitt County 83
Dibol 88
Distinguished Flying Cross 148
domestic 103
Drawhorn, Thomas 149
Dugat, Henry 79
Dykes, Norman 96

E

East Baytown 62
Eastern Star 90
Eastgate 20, 21, 55, 67, 117
Eastgate Road 55
Eaton, Pomella 138
Edgar family 48
Edgar, Lottie Martin 48
Edgar, R.B. 48, 79
Edmund E. and Nida Smith Jones Public Library 38, 54, 69
Edward Jones Company 129
Egg Circle 44, 72
Eggleston, Ricky 97
election 89, 91
Ellington Field 68, 126
Ellis, J.H.H. 29
El Paso 137
Enron Corporation 97
Entzminger, Ben 38
Entzminger, Jessie Baker 52
Esperson Dome Oil Field 82
evangelist 147
Exxon Mobil 126

F

Fairlawn Cemetery. 122
farmer 75, 87, 109, 112, 113, 119
farming 83, 149
farm laborer 106
Federal Land Bank of Houston Board 116
ferry 87, 146
fighter pilot 118
Fightin' Texas Aggie Band 125, 128
fire chief 127
fire marshal 84
First Avenue 63
First Baptist Church 19, 20, 29, 31, 32, 84, 102, 122, 130
First Liberty National Bank 103
First Street 29, 91
First United Methodist Church 29, 35, 38, 57, 67, 68, 99, 101, 104, 116, 125, 127, 167
Flowers family 56
Flowers, Jack 56
football player 129
Ford Avenue 98, 119
Ford, Dorothy Russell 100
Ford, Ella Fay King 57
Ford family 57, 58, 98
Fordland Estates subdivision 98
Ford, Milo, Sr. 33, 57, 98
Ford, M.W., Jr. 58, 98, 132
Ford, R.N. 91, 101
Ford Road 58
Forest Park Cemetery 65, 84
Fort Bend, Texas 111
forts 137
Fort Sam Houston 98
Fort Sam Houston National Cemetery 148
Fort Worth 63
Fourth Avenue 147
Fouts, John Louis 142
Franklin Hardin Chapter of Daughters of the Republic of Texas 127
Frank's Cafe 90
Freeport, Texas 84
French Cemetery 87, 111, 113
French Settlement 21, 70, 109
Friedman, Elaine Watel 53
Friedman family 53, 99, 132
Friedman, Saul 132, 159, 160, 171
Friedman, Susan 132, 171
Friend, Harlan 38
Friery family 60
Friery, John C., Jr. 60

funeral business 126
funeral director 127

G

Gaillard, John 76
Galveston, Texas 25, 30, 126
Gano, Lloyd 38
Garden Club 102
General Crude Oil Company 82
Gibson, Andy 88
Gilbert, Lloyd 131
Gilley's 95
Glass family 61
Glass, Melinda "Lindy" 61
Glenwood Cemetery 24, 114
Golden Rule 95
Goodrum family 20
Goose Creek 106, 107
Gordon, Reverend A.W. 33
Gosse family 118
Gosse, George 118
Gosse, Mary Elizabeth Schneider 118
governor of Texas 24, 114
Grace Community Baptist Church 78
Grantham, Edith 73
Graves, Blackie 96
Graves, Will 16, 28, 124
Green, Bernice 141
Grimes County 83
Groesbeck, Texas 77
Guadalcanal 61, 130, 144
Guam 144
Guice, J.L. 91, 101
Guiger Field, Washington 63
Gulf of Mexico 29
Gulf States Utilities 133
Gum Island 123
Gum Street 64
gunners mate 129

H

Haggerty, Thomas J. 112
Handbook of Texas 39
Haracek family 94
Hardin 121
hardware store 84
Harmon family 63, 64
Harmon, Geater 63
Harris, Bobby 70, 88, 93, 107, 115, 120, 138, 143, 145, 159, 163, 165, 168, 169, 170, 172, 173
Harrisburg 66
Harris County 20, 56, 79, 101, 106, 143
Harris, Joe, III 88, 107, 120, 143, 145
Harris, Joseph Denton, Jr. 115, 143
Harris, Larry 23
Harris, Linda Blackburn 38
Harrison, Nina 96
Hemphill, Reverend Lee 130
Hempstead 26
Henrich, Chris 88
Henry, Marvin 39, 107, 145
Henry, Paul J. 104
Hensarling, Ruth 123
Heritage Manor Nursing Home 93
Heritage Villa Nursing and Rehab Center 93
Highland Cemetery, Oklahoma 76
Hightower, Lockhart 89
Hill, Alma Lindemann 65
Hill family 64
Hill, K.C. 64
historical markers 28
historic downtown 91
Hogue, W.S. 29
Holbrook, Chester 15, 28, 54, 65, 72, 82, 120, 124, 133
Holbrook, Ellen Nelson 15, 29, 54, 65, 73

Holbrook family 15, 28, 54, 66, 73
Holbrook & Graves Contractors 124
Holbrook subdivision 15, 28, 65, 72
Holitzke family 67
Holitzke, Joseph 67
Holitzke, Mary Ann Navatil 68
Holmes family 68
Holmes, Johnnie Lee 68
home builder 108
home laundress 111
homemaker 116, 120, 134
Honolulu Memorial 57, 74
Hood's Brigade 112
Hooks 149
horse racing 27
Houston Astros 105
Houston Baptist University 97
Houston Club 102
Houston Dispatch 114
Houston National Bank 75, 114
Houston Optimist Club 114
Houston Post 114
Houston, Sam 24, 25, 26, 69, 146
Houston Street 35, 103, 119, 140
Houston, Texas 36, 39, 54, 65, 66, 67, 68, 69, 73, 75, 88, 95, 97, 99, 100, 113, 114, 115, 120, 126, 132, 138
Hudson Motor Car Dealership 133
Huffman 56, 100
Huffman Cemetery 19
humane officer 79
Humble 56, 71
Humble High School 55
Humble Oil and Refining Company 24, 62, 89, 98, 114, 125, 126, 127
Hunnicutt, Anna Slade 69
Hunnicutt family 70
Hunnicutt Hotel 70
Hunnicutt, J.D. 69, 76
Hurricane Ike 107
Hydril Company 67

I

independence from Mexico 118
Independence Street 60
Iowa 15, 22, 57, 66, 115
Irion County 26
Iverson, Neal 120

J

Jamison, Allene Solomon 70, 113, 120, 134, 145
Jamison, Bob 134
Jamison family 70, 136
Jamison Insurance Agency 71
Jamison, J.B. 38
Jamison, Mary Beth 169, 170, 172, 173
Jamison, W.B. 84
Jamison, W.T. 33, 70, 113, 120, 134, 145
janitor 79
Jansen, Eugene 65
Jefferson County 81, 104, 106
John Sealy College of Nursing 126
Johnson County 74
Johnson family 58
Johnson, Jessica Ford 58, 98
Johnson, John 58, 98
Johnson, Reverend Jerry 122
Jones, Reverend A.D. 90
Jordan, Reverend J.L. 20
Journal-Advance 80
justice of the peace 106

K

Kaplan, Dr. Allan 132
Karnes, Texas 64
Kay, Clyde D. 73
Kay family 73

Kay, Seth 120
Kay Street 125
Kelly family 101
Kemah, Texas 39, 57
Kenefick 100
Kentucky Derby of Dayton 119
Kerr, A.E. 49, 74, 79
Kerr family 75
Kerrville 97, 100
Key family 83
Kids' Day 119
Kimmie Brown Elementary School 23
Kindt, Abraham F. 75
Kindt family 75
Kindt subdivision 76
King George 148
Klemp Corporation 76
Kline's Grocery 93

L

LaCour, Carey 79, 122
LaCour family 79, 122
LaCour, Will 122
Ladd, E.P., Sr. 49, 79
Ladd family 80
Ladd, Josie Phillips 80
Ladd, Myrtle Lou 81
LaFitte, Jean 25
Laird family 82
Laird, Mary 82
Laird, Morgan 28, 82
Lakata Club 127
Lamar College 117
Lamb (Hightower) 135, 142
land developer 108
Landwehr, Pat 18
La Porte, Texas 114, 144
Lauderdale family 77
Lavaca County 64
law practice 136
Lawrence family 83
Lawrence Street 28, 145
Lawrence, Teresa 84
Lawrence, Winnefred Key 82
Lawson, Alice Prater 111
Lawson, Brayboy 111
Lawson family 111
Lawson, Sherial 110
lawyer 97
Lea, Reverend J.A. 27
LeBlanc family 77
LeBlanc, June 77
LeBlanc, Mary Lauderdale 77
Lee College 144
Libertad Chapter of the Daughters of the American Revolution 127
Liberty 17, 35, 38, 54, 60, 68, 73, 78, 87, 88, 89, 94, 98, 102, 108, 121, 128, 134, 136, 138, 140
Liberty Avenue 36
Liberty Catholic Hospital 108
Liberty Chamber of Commerce 122
Liberty County 15, 22, 23, 24, 25, 26, 33, 62, 65, 66, 75, 87, 89, 91, 104, 106, 111, 121, 146, 148, 152, 160, 161, 162, 163, 166, 167, 168, 170, 171, 172, 173, 174
Liberty County A&M Mother's Club 127
Liberty County Courthouse 30, 75, 76
Liberty County Jail 90
Liberty County sheriff 89
Liberty County Sheriff's Department 120
Liberty Lass 148
Liberty Middle School 88
Liberty National Bank 107, 145

Liberty Vindicator 15, 28, 32, 66, 98, 101, 161, 162, 163, 167, 170, 171, 172, 173, 174
Liberty Volunteers 26
Ligons, Dennis, Sr. 85
Ligons family 85
Ligons, Mary Lee Love 85
Lindsey, Johnny 77
Linnemann family 65
Linney 107
Linney Cemetery 20, 29, 57, 70, 87, 96, 101, 104, 118, 119, 120
Linney Creek 87, 121
Linney Creek subdivision 16, 100, 101, 110, 113, 121, 122
Linney, Elizabeth Weeks 86
Linney family 86, 112
Linney Hill 120
Linney, Michael 86
Little Rock Automobile Company 80
Lockett, Annette 111
Logan, Captain William M. 26
Lone Star Beer Distributing Company 16, 133
Lorraine American Cemetery 17
Louisiana and Western Railroad 118
Louisiana Rodeo Hall of Fame 94
Lovell's Lake 98
Lovers Lane 37
Lowe, Delia Berry 89
Lowe family 89
Lowe, Leona 90
Lowe Oil Company 90
Lowe, Pat 89
Lowe, Reverend Robert B. 34
Lower Trinity Valley Conservation District 127
Lowery, W.S. 30
Lowe's Town House and Motel 90
Lowe Woods 36
Luke Street 88
lumber company 79
lumber manufacturing 80

M

Madisonville, Texas 60, 73
Magnolia Cemetery Association 116
Magnolia Oil Service Station 133
Magnolia Park Cemetery 16, 20, 23, 29, 58, 64, 67, 72, 78, 82, 117, 132, 134, 144
Magnolia Place Care Center 78
Main Street 103, 119, 125, 137, 138, 143, 145
Mama Lucy 95
manager of City Water Works 84
Manila American Cemetery 61
marshal 91
Marshall County 19
Martin, Bishop Paul E. 34
Martin, Bob 120
Martin, Clarence 103
Martin, Kathryn Shanks 119
Marwick's Accounting Firm 97
Mason 114, 136
Masonic Lodge 16, 90, 122
Matagorda Bay 136
Mathinson, Dr. Ed M. 34
mayor of Dayton 88, 91, 100, 125, 127
McBride, Joe 95
McBride, Lucy 95
McDowell, Myron 149
McLenda Ford Company 54
McLeod family 19
McLeod, J.F. 19, 30
MDAnderson Cancer Center 105
Meadows subdivision 95
Merrett, Mildred 98
Merrett, Peter 88
Merrill Lynch 132

Merritt family 98
Merritt, William H., III 98
Methodist Episcopal Church 29, 32, 33, 71, 100, 106, 134
Methodist minister 71
Mexia 116
Mexican government 25, 86
Mexican War 137
midwife 61
Milby High School 66
Miller, Rebecca Friedman 99
Mineral Wells 116
missionaries 18
Mission, Texas 63
M&M Beauty Shop 98
Moller, C.M. 91, 101
Moller, Laura Alice White 101
Mont Belvieu 28, 123
Montgomery County 16
Montgomery Tribune 81
Moore, Johnny 77
Moore, Sue 77
Moore, W.C. 19, 30
Moreau, Clayton 36
Moreau family 36
Moreau, Mrs. Leo 74
Mt. Pleasant Baptist Church 85, 95
Munson League 21, 119
museum 119
musician 72
music teacher 125
Muttonhead 93

N

Nacogdoches 25, 88, 131
Nacogdoches County 25
Nacogdoches High School 131
Nacogdoches-Lynchberg Trail 39
National Honor Society 96, 97
Navasota, Texas 20
Neel, W.S. 91
Nelson family 15, 22, 66
Nelson, Joe 15, 66
Neuman, E.B., II 63, 123
Neuman family 94
Neuman, Judy Robinson 95
Neuman Motor Company 63
Neuman, Mutt 93
Neuman's Gulf Service Station 95
Newton County 104
Nigton, Texas 85
1900 storm 30
Nome 122
Norcross family 104, 106
Norcross, Frank 105
Norcross Grocery 105
Norcross, Lucy Tilton 105
Norcross, Milton 104
Norcross, Nellie Wright 104
Norcross, Truett 103
Norcross, Zoe 105
Normanna, Texas 83
Nottingham, Fredda 131
nursing 126

O

Oak Leaf Clusters 17, 68, 118
Oak Street 145
Obschestvo Remeslenago Truda (ORT) 54
offshore drilling 62
oil boom 89
oil business 126
oil field 62
oil field mud business 121
oil industry 114
oil production 114
Old River Community 145
Old School 119
Old School Museum 69, 84, 108

Old Spanish Trail Highway 137
Old Spanish Trail (OST) 69, 137
Old Tram Road 141
O'Neil, Billy 98
Orange 125, 133
organist 100, 127
Oyster Creek 70

P

Pace-Stancil Funeral Home 127
Palms Memorial Park Cemetery 127, 128
parent-teacher association 49, 70
Parker, David 108, 110, 144
Parker family 108
Pasadena, Texas 15, 39, 66
Pathways Youth and Family Services 97
Paul, Ed 109
Paul family 95, 109
Paul, Joann 85, 95
Paul, Pearl Cabello 109
Payne, Beatrice 95
Pearl Harbor 126
Pecanwood Mobile Home Park 96
Pelco Construction Company 143
Pelly 61
Peoples Building Center 143
Peoples Feed Store 143
Peoples Lumber and Feed Company 143
Pershing, General John 138
Phillips 66 90
pianist 73, 100, 125, 129
Pickett, H.W. 29
Pine Bluff (Arkansas) Auto Club 80
Pine Place subdivision 110
Pine Street 145
pipe organ 127
Pleasant Hill Baptist Church 61, 90, 123
Point Barrow 145
Port Boliver 88
postmaster 146
Post Office Avenue 23
Prater, Dennis, Sr. 110
Prater, Melinda 110
preachers 19
Presidential Unit Citation 68, 118
principal 96
Priscilla Club 72, 127
Production National Life Insurance Board 116
Professional Bull Riders Association 95
Provost, Hurley 79
Pruett, Edmund 111
Pruett family 111
Pruett, Lucinda Abshier 112
Pruett, Minnie Day 113
Pruitt, Ed, Jr. 57
Pure Oil Company 100
Purple Heart 57, 68, 74, 130

Q

Queen Elizabeth 148

R

railroad 39, 55, 56, 65, 115, 124, 140, 143, 153
ranching 57, 71, 109
Ratliff, A.S. 91
reading teacher 96
Real Estate Broker 108
Reconstruction 27
Red Cross 126
registered nurse 126
Republic of Texas 146
rice dryer 16, 115

rice farming 15, 28, 57, 66, 115, 133
Rice University 99
Richter, Alphene 18, 37
Richter, Dr. Ernest 18, 37, 127
Rio Grande Valley 102
Rio Movie Theater 24, 93
Rizzo family 73
Rizzo, Juanita Holbrook 16, 28, 54, 72
Rizzo, Sam 73
Robert and Lillian Parker Meeting Room 108
Roberts, Bobby 107, 145
Roberts, Nancy 103
rodeo 94
Rodessa High School 148
Rosswood 135
Rotary Club of Dayton 108
Rotary Club of Liberty 122
Royal Canadian Air Force 147
R.S. Sterling Investment Company 114
Runyan, A.W. 33
Rutt, C.L. 142
Ryan Cemetery 28, 68, 90

S

Saipan 74
Sam Houston National Cemetery 98
Sam Houston Normal Institute, 71
Sam Rayborn Lake 96
San Antonio 26, 96, 98, 137, 138, 148
Sanders, Bobby 18
Sanders, Carl 18
Sanders, Else Zachariah 18
Sanders family 18
San Felipe 26
San Jacinto Methodist Hospital Board of Directors 116
San Jacinto River 55
San Patricio County 84
Santa Anna 118
Savings and Loan officer 108
sawmill 48, 90, 115, 142, 143
schoolteacher 23, 57, 88, 131
Seaberg family 22, 115
Seaberg, Juanita Addington 116
Seaberg Rice, Inc. 116
Seaberg, Roy, Sr. 115
Second Avenue 17
Second Street 91
Seekamp family 117
Seekamp, LaVergne Whittle 117
Seekamp, Vernon 117
Shanks, Dick 119
Shanks family 118
Shanks, Frances Marion 119
Shanks, Granville 118
Shanks' Hill 119
Shanks, Mary Gosse 118
Shanks, Thelma Fingleman 119
Shaw, T.H. 33, 101
Sheaf, The 49, 70
Shell Oil Company 17
Shell Oil Exploration Company 120
Sheperd, Texas 25
Sheppard Air Force Base 63
sheriff 89
Sherman family 126
Sherwood Drive 88
Sherwood subdivision 88, 120
Silver Plaque 147
Simmons, C.H. 30
Simmons, John 23
Sinclair Oil 116
Sjolander, Bill 23
Slade family 70
slaves 27, 146
Slover family 121
Slover, Myra Kelly 16, 101
Slover, Roy 16, 101, 121

Smith, Bishop Frank 33
Smith, D.E., Jr. 134
Smith, Everlean 79
Smith family 79, 122
Smith, Frances Holt 26
Smith, Mamie LaCour 79, 122
Smith, Pleasant L. 122
Snuggle Inn 36
Solomon family 71
Sons of Confederate Veterans 127
Sons of the American Revolution 127
Sons of the Republic of Texas 127
Sour Lake 113
Southern Industrial and Lumber Review 48, 135, 159
Southern Methodist University 54, 73
Southern Pacific Railroad 62, 112, 114, 115, 118, 143
South Pacific 144
South Texas Hardwood Company 79, 143
South Town League 38
Southwestern Baptist Theological Seminary 102
Southwestern Louisiana Institute 147
soybean farmer 116
soybeans 122
Spears, Nora 31
St. Anne's Catholic Cemetery 55
St. Anne's Catholic Church 55
State Highway 3 138
State Highway 146 140
State Highway 321 37, 56, 103, 109
Stephen F. Austin Elementary 38, 96
Stephen F. Austin State College 131
Stephen F. Austin State University 88
Stephens, Steve 88
Sterling, Ben 123, 125
Sterling, Betty Sherman 123, 125
Sterling family 23, 24, 113, 123, 125, 128, 151, 152, 169, 170, 171
Sterling Funeral Home 125
Sterling, James Bennett, Sr. 125
Sterling, J.B. 33
Sterling, Jim 23, 122, 125, 132
Sterling, Jimmy 123, 125
Sterling, Karen Hinton 128
Sterling, Linda Harding 129
Sterling, Lulu Crites 24
Sterling, Maud Gage 114
Sterling, O.B., Sr. 23
Sterling Oil and Refining Company 114, 129
Sterling, Ophelia Dodd 125
Sterling Realty 128
Sterling, Ross, Sr. 24, 49, 62, 71, 75, 79, 91, 113, 125, 143, 169
Sterling, Sandra Kittrell 128
Sterling Street 24
Stevens, Adelene 124
Stevens, Ray 129
Stieler family 97
Stieler, Justin 97
Stieler, Meredith Voytek 96
Stilson Community 57, 115
Stitch and Chatter Club 72, 127
St. Joseph's Catholic Church 38
St. Mary's Law School 96
stockbroker 129
Stock Law 109
stock raiser 87
Stoesser, Mrs. Emil Joseph 31
Stone Creek Homes 88
Stone, Dollie Thames 131
Stone family 131
Stone, Howard 131
St. Paul AME Church 103
student council 129
subdivision developer 28
submarine 57
Suburban Acres subdivision 70, 72, 113, 120, 134, 136, 145

Sunday school superintendent 95
Sunday school teacher 127
Supreme Court 76
Susan Street 87

T

Tabbs Bay 62
Tablets of the Missing 57, 130
Tadlock, Dr. J.T. 33, 100
Tallow Wood Trail 23
Tarkington 90
Tarkington Prairie 26, 68, 89
Tasso Country 109
Taylor, Ellis 16, 133
Taylor, Gertie 133
teaching 72
Teague 116
telegraph operator 65, 70
telephone operator 77, 116
Temple, Texas 64
Texaco Oil Company 119
Texarkana 149
Texas A&M 15, 37, 97, 125, 127, 128, 129
Texas and New Orleans Railroad 33, 118, 135
Texas Avenue 73
Texas Christian University 114
Texas City disaster 126, 127
Texas Department of Transportation 138
Texas High School Coaches' Association 60
Texas Highway Department 56, 60, 123
Texas Independence 61
Texas Infantry 112
Texas Revolution 26, 86
Texas Rice Council Board 116
Texas Rice Improvement Association Board 116
Texas Runaway Scrape 118
Texas University 147
Texas Women's University 53
Third Avenue 129
Thomaston, Texas 83
Tillman family 96
Tillman, Marcia Voytek 96
Tillman, Rix Thomas 96
Tilton family 106
Toledo Bend Lake 96
Tom Green County 26
tourist courts 90
Town Center 143
Town & Country Realty 108
trade routes 137
train depot 70
Travis, Colonel William B. 26
Treetop Terrace subdivision 121
Tri County Lumber Company 102, 121
Trinity Development Company 82, 107, 145
Trinity River 25, 87, 140, 145
Trinity Valley Exposition 127
Trinity Valley & Northern Railroad 115, 135, 142, 143
Trousdale family 93
truck farm 106
tuberculosis 99
Tucker family 136
Tucker, Mary Damek 136
Tucker, Robert S. 77, 136
Tucker, Tom 136
Turner, Martha Ann 130
Tyler County 56

U

Union Church 30
Union Pacific Railroad 39
United Methodist Church 35
University of Arizona 132
University of Louisiana 147
University of Texas 96, 121
University of Texas Medical Branch 126
University of Texas Medical Branch School of Nursing 126
USAF U.S. Temporary Cemetery in British New Guinea 64
U.S. Air Force 67, 99, 118, 144
U.S. Army 17, 60, 63, 68, 133
U.S. Army Air Corps 67, 148
U.S. Highway 90 37, 69, 77, 90, 95, 119, 123
U.S. highway system 138
U.S. Marine Corps 73, 144
U.S. Navy 129, 132
USS *Pickerel* 57

V

vacation Bible school 127
Valley Players 54
Victoria High School 117
Victoria, Texas 117
Vietnam 144
Voytek family 96
Voytek, Sandra 96, 124

W

Waco Street 38, 115, 135
Waldrop, Allan 66
Waldrop, Evelyn Holbrook 16, 28, 54
Waldrop Ford Company 54
Waldrop, Nelson 54
Walker family 90
Walker, Luke 90
Walker, Maud Dunlap 90
Wallace, T.H. 38
Waller County 19
War Department 68, 74
Waring family 143
Waring Street 95
Waring, Willie 143
waterworks superintendent 84
Webb, Reverend William C. 35
well digger 109
Wells Cemetery 36
West family 144
West Liberty 25, 86, 87, 112, 118, 142
West, Randy 108, 144
West, Sue Copeland 144
Westwood Street 108
White family 101
White, Roxy Line 26
Whitten, Reverend T.B. 33
Whittington, Nell 105, 107
Wichita Falls, Texas 63, 116
Wilson, Charles 30, 33
Wilson family 87
Wilson, Lisa 87
Wilson's Church 29, 30
Wilson, Troy 93
Winfree 28, 57, 65, 72, 73, 94, 140
Winfree, A.B.J. 145
Winfree, Benjamin 145
Winfree, Charlotte Millard 146
Winfree family 145
Winfree, Jacob Freland 146
Winfree, Mary 146
Winfree, Mary Catherin Fisher 146
Winfree, Philip 145
Winfree Road 54
Winfree's Cove 146
Winfree Street 77
Winfree, Zachary Taylor 146
Wingo, Annie 79, 122
Wisegerber, Betty Jo 56, 69

Wisegerber, Lester Ray 55, 69, 119
Wolf Island Road 65
World War I 64, 84, 89, 101, 106, 138
World War II 17, 23, 56, 60, 63, 67, 68, 72, 73, 98, 115, 117, 125, 126, 129, 143, 147
Wright family 104
Wycliff, Emily 61
Wycliff, Wilbert 61

Y

Young, Bubba 147
Young, Cy 23
Young family 147
Young, R.V. 39

Z

Zbranek, Zeke 120
Zylks, Bobbie Alford 148
Zylks family 148
Zylks, Pete 148

ABOUT THE AUTHOR

Caroline Stansell Wadzeck devoted thirty-eight years to the field of education, first as a classroom teacher and then thirty-three years as a school librarian. Her goal was to instill the love of reading in her students. She received Teacher of the Year honors at both school districts for which she worked: Dayton ISD and Barbers Hill ISD. She received the Hotho Award from the Texas Library Association for her creative programs that encouraged reading and was named a TLA Tall Texan. In "retirement," she serves as co-curator of Dayton's Old School Museum and president of the Jones Public Library Board and is an active member of the Dayton Historical Society, the Mu Iota Chapter of the Delta Kappa Gamma Society International and the Lakata Club. When she's not actively pursuing historical data about her community or family, she enjoys spending time with her four grandchildren and traveling with her husband, Larry. They reside in Dayton, Texas.

Visit us at
www.historypress.net

This title is also available as an e-book